Housing: Where's the Plan?

PERSPECTIVES

Series editor: Diane Coyle

Housing: Where's the Plan?

Kate Barker

LONDON PUBLISHING PARTNERSHIP

Published by London Publishing Partnership
www.londonpublishingpartnership.co.uk

Published in association with
Enlightenment Economics
www.enlightenmenteconomics.com

ISBN: 978-1-907994-11-1 (pbk)

A catalogue record for this book is
available from the British Library

This book has been composed in Candara

Copy-edited and typeset by
T&T Productions Ltd, London
www.tandtproductions.com

Cover art by Kate Prentice

Contents

Preface

Housing matters. We all need a home and we all want to live in a pleasant place. We talk about the housing market endlessly. But too few people really understand the underlying economics of the market and how housing interacts with finance, planning and taxation.

The last major review of UK housing supply, which I led, was published just over a decade ago. Its key contention – that the UK (particularly England) needed to build homes at a faster rate – was controversial at the time but has since become widely accepted. And yet the number of homes built in England from 2010 to 2013 was less than half the official estimate of how many more households would want to find somewhere to live. The signs are that 2014 will have seen increased homebuilding, but still far short of what is needed. Why is this, and shouldn't more be done to fix the housing market? Isn't the solution still building more housing in areas where people want to live?

The recent shortage of supply has exacerbated some underlying problems. England has a relatively old stock of housing – some in poor condition and much of it in areas where the economy is now weaker, as economic activity is becoming increasingly concentrated in the South East. Empty homes are also often to be found in these less prosperous parts of the country. Yet local opposition and the failure of many local authorities to produce up-to-date plans for their area has led to a persistent undersupply of homes in much of southern England.

This means there is increasing inequality between those who are able to become homebuyers (often aided by parents who already have a stake in the housing market) and those who cannot afford to leave the private rented sector. Undersupply also contributes to volatility in house prices – illustrated by the quick pick-up in prices in 2013 when it became easier to get a mortgage. In London the price rises were very rapid, though this was due in large part to rising demand from wealthy individuals from outside the UK.

The financial crisis was clearly the major factor behind this latest period of low supply. Housing demand was strongly suppressed as the recession took its toll on household incomes. In addition, UK banks cut back on their mortgage lending and, with belated caution, asked for larger deposits. House prices fell sharply in 2008–9 and were then relatively stable before starting to climb again during 2013.

Falling prices during the downturn hit housebuilders hard, as the land they had bought at pre-crisis prices suddenly became worth much less. With cash flow also hit as fewer homes were sold, many small and medium-sized builders went out of business. Several lean years have also weakened the skills and materials base for the industry, and it is likely to be some time before new supply returns to pre-crisis levels.

Even at the pre-crisis peak, the rate of new housing supply was not enough to meet demand pressures in England – demand increases due to population growth and increasing incomes. If supply does not respond sufficiently to demand, then the outcome is obvious: prices rise and, what is worse, they are expected to continue rising. This means there is a big incentive for those who can afford it to invest in housing, while others get left further and further behind.

Housing affordability can be a misused term (indeed, I have misused it myself). It can be hard to get a mortgage due to the requirement for a large deposit and the new requirement to verify a reliable income. But once in home ownership, if the mortgage can be sustained, rising prices and favourable tax treatment mean that over the long term the costs of ownership can be quite low. It is often tenants, faced with rising rents, who really have an affordability problem.

In my housing supply review ten years ago, I pointed out that many people gain from an undersupply of housing: landowners and homeowners see the value of their assets rising, and local authorities gain from their ability to request that developers provide more infrastructure. But there are losers today: those who pay higher rents and are simply priced out of home ownership. And in the long run we all lose: there are economic costs as workers find it harder to move job around the country, the housing market is more volatile, we have a high level of household debt, which makes the economy harder to manage, and investment is diverted to too great an extent into the stock of bricks and mortar. But it is hard for people to perceive the underlying longer-term costs that are paid by everyone. Planning decisions therefore tend to give too much weight to the visible, local costs and too little to the wider and longer-term national benefits.

There are of course costs from building more homes. The most obvious is the loss of open space. This often accounts for much of the local resistance to development, alongside worries about the strain on infrastructure. But there are also very important issues concerning the balance of economic activity around England, water supply, biodiversity and other environmental pressures that require a response at a regional or national level. (At local level, it is often possible for a new development to be carried out in a manner that enhances some aspects of the environment.)

And the housing market is inherently difficult to manage. Inevitably, property is part of a household's financial planning – it is mainly a home but it is also an investment. We take on a lot of debt to finance house purchase, which makes families vulnerable if they face a shock that reduces their income. This also means that the government needs to be cautious about any housing-related tax changes in order to avoid major market disruption.

There have been positive policy developments, though, some of which began a decade ago with a stronger focus on local land supply for housing, and over time these policies will ameliorate housing-market problems. In particular, the National Planning Policy Framework has given real impetus to local authorities to put plans in place, and planning inspectors now have the ability to ensure that these plans provide for enough new homes. Following the financial crisis, the new Financial Policy Committee at the Bank of England has powers to curb potentially reckless lending, which should limit housing market volatility.

But there are some big concerns too. The government now has a long-term role in shared equity via the Help to Buy scheme. As one prominent commentator put it:

> The government has increased its commitment to frighteningly expensive housing. It is a trap from which the UK may not now escape.[1]

And the policy changes we've seen will not completely resolve the fundamentally intractable issues discussed in this book. It sets out the history of these problems and describes how the planning system, local democracy, the tax system and wealth distribution all set the framework and incentives that drive the behaviours of developers, landowners and households.

Government faces very uncomfortable choices. The housing outcomes described above are bad for many in private renting, they are bad for many young families desperate for more space, and they are damaging to the wider economy. A housing stock that is becoming ever more expensive overall, and which is not located where it is needed, results in sharp divergences in the distribution of wealth and opportunity between generations, and between those living in different areas. To create a fairer and less harmful housing market, a combination of strong central direction about housing supply and unpopular taxation changes would be required. But politicians find it hard to grasp these nettles: there is far too much short-term pain and the gain will go to their successors. It is easier for them to carry on with somewhat ineffective knee-jerk and populist help for first-time buyers.

We need to have a clearer analysis of the choices, particularly with regard to the environmental issues. The word 'sustainability' needs a national focus – it cannot be fully assessed locally. Are there actually serious environmental or social costs to developing more homes in London and the South East, and, if so, what would the economic cost of a different distribution of population be? The values and trade-offs implicit in planning policy should be made more transparent. We protect open land now by paying a very high price for the space for housing – but this trade-off is rarely explicitly discussed.

We should accept that the housing market cannot be made perfect. This book will suggest criteria for judging what a better housing market looks like. But these criteria can conflict, and people will come to different conclusions. Some would regard more new homes around the economic hot spot of

Cambridge as a success, for example, while others would view it as environmentally damaging.

I have become less convinced that it will be possible to build enough to meet demand in much of southern England, given the strength of local opposition in many places. So building more housing will not be the only answer. We will also need to ameliorate the consequences of demand continuing to exceed the available supply.

What policies are needed now? The proposals I set out include the following.

- A clear view in government of environmental and social costs, influencing spatial planning at the national level, and leading the debate about where new towns are placed and about major urban extensions.
- A strong national influence over local planning decisions, in part to ensure better cooperation between local authorities. But a further radical reform of planning now would be unhelpful.
- Much vacant land is in the hands of public bodies. We need to get these sites into use, which may include a greater role for local authorities in buying and preparing sites.
- Financial compensation for those adversely affected by new development.
- The introduction of capital gains tax on main residences, among other tax changes.

Finally, the big impediment to this kind of package is that housing policy is currently split among several government departments and independent regulators. Some roles should be consolidated, and priorities clearly identified. If we cannot have a unified approach to the proposals set out above, housing market policies will remain incoherent and the housing crisis will deepen each year.

Acknowledgements

I am very grateful to the many people with whom I have discussed housing issues over the last decade, particularly Paul Chamberlain, Paul Cheshire, Kelvin MacDonald, Steve Nickell, Henry Overman, Pete Redfern, Lord Matthew Taylor, Robert Upton and Christine Whitehead. I am also indebted to Diane Coyle for giving me the chance to think all this through again and to Sam Clark for being such a supportive editor.

Chapter 1

What outcomes
do we want?

Since the financial crisis of 2007–9, discussion of a 'housing crisis' has been growing and a range of policy responses have been put forward. For example, the mortgage guarantee scheme introduced in late 2013 as the second part of 'Help to Buy' was intended to help kick-start sluggish housing transactions, while the so-called bedroom tax introduced in April 2013 reduced housing benefit for those with spare bedrooms in an effort to cut the growing housing benefit bill. By mid 2014, the primary concern was the overheating market in London and its hinterland. But these policy responses and debates don't effectively tackle the big underlying issues that have emerged over recent decades, including a widening gulf in wealth between those in owner-occupation and those out of it, and the resulting concerns about inequality between generations.

Governments are rarely precise in how they measure their success with regard to the housing market. In 2007, the Labour government summed up its aspirations as follows:

> We want everyone to have access to a decent home at a price they can afford, in a place where they want to live and work.[2]

It would be possible to measure the success of the first part of this goal, but the second part may not even be feasible.

The housing goals of the 2010 coalition government, as stated on the website of the Department for Communities and Local Government, have varied. The 2013 version included 'helping more people to buy a home', which might imply that one criterion for success would be a higher rate of owner-occupation. This has been an implicit or explicit policy goal for governments of all persuasions since the 1970s. But many other goals are pursued by governments, including managing house price inflation if it signals an unsustainable boom, or not building on green belt or environmentally sensitive land. Achieving success in terms of any of these aims requires (among other things) some myth busting.

Is more home ownership desirable?

Long-term policy support for home ownership has been quite successful. The share of owner-occupation in England rose pretty steadily between 1961, when it stood at 44%, and 1991, when it reached 68%. That level changed little until the financial crisis. So, while in 2001 the share of owner-occupied households reached 70%, after 2007 that share fell, to 64% by 2012. Table 1.1 indicates that the rise in owner-occupation in the 1960s and 1970s reflected a move out of the private rented sector, whereas in the 1980s and 1990s it was the share of social housing that fell. The post-crisis fall in owner-occupation has been offset by a move back into the private rented sector: its share has risen from around 10% in the early 2000s to over 18% in 2012.

It is argued that a high level of home ownership leads to better care of the housing stock, and more commitment by households[3] to their community. While this might be true, homeowners also tend to be better off and better educated,

Table 1.1. Changes in share of household tenure (England).

	Owner-occupied	Social rent	Private rent
1961	43.9	24.5	31.6
1971	52.4	28.3	19.3
1981	58.4	30.5	11.1
1991	67.6	23.0	9.4
2001	69.7	20.2	10.1
2007	68.0	17.7	14.3
2012	64.2	17.3	18.5

Source: Department of Communities and Local Government.

Myth 1 The UK has an unusually high rate of owner-occupation

In 2012, among other EU countries, only Germany (53%) and Austria (57%) had an appreciably lower rate of owner-occupation than the UK, according to Eurostat figures. In both Italy and Spain the rate is around 75%. However, the proportion of owner-occupiers in the UK who have a mortgage on their property is comparatively high and we still have a somewhat above-average proportion of households in social rented housing. The share of the private rented sector is a little lower than the EU average (notably, Germany and the Netherlands have bigger private rented sector shares).

which might contribute to these behavioural effects. There is not enough evidence to disparage tenants' public spiritedness. But housing tenure can have social consequence. In the

US context, Anne Shlay has commented that home owner-ship is

> not simply an indicator of social inequality; it is a causal mechanism underlying inequality. Also important is housing tenure's role as a basis for solidifying divisions and antipa-thies among different social groups.[4]

There are also economic arguments *against* too high a rate of home ownership.[5] The most important is that a high rate of home ownership tends to reduce labour mobility, and so makes it more difficult for adjustment to take place following economic shocks, such as a recession. Young people may find it harder to leave home to look for work if there is a thin or ex-pensive rental market. The scale of these effects is uncertain, however, and it is obviously not solely home ownership that makes people reluctant to move but also attachment to an area or family ties.

Another important consideration is that a high rate of owner-occupation increases opposition to new residential building, because this is perceived to reduce the value of existing homes. For many households, the home is the largest single investment, so it is not surprising that new develop-ment proposals arouse strong emotions.

If neither social nor economic arguments for a high rate of home ownership are compelling, why does this tenure so often receive special treatment? The obvious answer is that in the UK it remains the long-term aspiration of the majority. The Council of Mortgage Lenders has drawn together a se-quence of surveys (conducted since the mid 1980s) that sug-gest that around 80% of households would prefer to be home-owners within a decade. There was only a slight decline in this proportion after the financial crisis, despite the initial fall in house prices. Governments want to be seen to support this aspiration but they are hampered in their ability to do so by the paradox that while it is easier for first-time buyers if house prices are lower, falling house prices are obviously unpopular with the majority who already own a home. So governments resort to measures to subsidize ownership. These help some people but fail to tackle the underlying problems in the housing market, and they can therefore have an adverse impact on other households by pushing prices higher.

Building more homes is often an unattractive option for politicians, especially at local level. The benefits of boosting supply only become apparent after a number of years but voters voice strong local opposition to building on specific sites today. Governments can most effectively rise to this challenge if they convey clear messages about why increased housing supply matters, and about the potential riskiness of home ownership. It is not for governments to prescribe the tenure mix we 'ought' to live in, and it's actually a bit odd that governments support our preference for home ownership: many households will have other economic aspirations too (owning a luxury car, for example), but we don't expect government policy to subsidize these.

Affordability

It is often asserted that housing is becoming 'unaffordable', usually on the basis of house prices relative to earnings. But care has to be taken when interpreting the facts here (see Figure 1.1). Dual-earner households can clearly afford more in mortgage payments, and interest rates have fallen, which makes the initial mortgage costs more affordable than they were in the 1970s or 1980s. Interest rates have fallen along with wage and price inflation, so the real cost of the capital

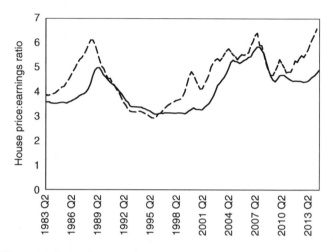

Figure 1.1. Ratio of average house price to average earnings for the UK (solid line) and for Greater London (dashed line). *Source*: Halifax House Price Index.

repayment of a mortgage has tended to rise. Lower interest rates and more dual-income households have not fully offset the rise in prices, which has resulted in a rise over time in the age of first-time buyers. Loan-to-income ratios for first-time buyers have been on a long-term upward trend. It is these long-term considerations that suggest a persistent failure of supply to keep pace with demand, although the underlying trends are not easy to separate from short-run volatility driven by changes in the price or availability of credit.

In addition, the upward trend in house prices relative to incomes, which has persisted for the past forty years, has resulted in a changed picture of wealth inequality. One effect has been to spread wealth further down the income distribution, which might be considered a good thing. But it has become harder for people who cannot become homeowners to accumulate wealth.

Myth 2 **Rising prices mean housing is unaffordable for all**

Once a household enters owner-occupation, the expectation of future house price rises actually means, despite cash-flow pressures from mortgage payments, that its housing costs are often rather cheap. It is those unable to access owner-occupation, who may well be paying higher rents, for whom housing is expensive.

The role of the private rented sector

Since the financial crisis, the private rented sector has come to play a larger role in the housing market, with more people having to opt for renting, rather than borrowing to buy a home. Two potentially incompatible policies have been proposed in response.

The first is to encourage the building of new private rented capacity to meet growing demand, as new supply from 'speculative' homebuilders collapsed after the financial crisis. In 2012, the Montague Review[6] proposed measures to encourage institutional investment in private rental. The government responded by offering finance for suitable proposals, which took some of the risk away from investors, and it also guaranteed debt used to fund new private rented sector schemes.

These measures should help, but institutional investors may still need to see capital appreciation because net rents (rents after management costs are subtracted) in the first decade of the 2000s produced a yield of only 3.5%. Buy-to-let landlords with only a few properties tend to undervalue their management time, giving them an apparently better yield and enabling them to undercut institutional investors.

Increased institutional investment in rental housing might therefore only be financially viable if potential landlords can acquire properties at slightly below-market prices.

This could be achieved by local authorities designating some land specifically for private rental building – annoying the landowner, who would then receive a slightly lower price because of the planning restriction – or reducing the affordable housing requirement and other planning obligations for private rented sector sites. In return, investors could be required to keep dwellings as rental properties for a specified number of years, with the added benefit that this would offer greater security of tenure to the tenant. But this raises some risks. In particular, if the private rented sector has expanded mainly because of mortgage market constraints, it is reasonable to expect the demand for rented accommodation to decline as the mortgage market recovers. If private rented units cannot be sold to prospective owner-occupiers, there would then be a risk of voids (periods of vacancy between tenants).

The second policy response has been to try to limit rent rises, which have been a major contributor to pushing up the housing benefit bill. Steps have been taken to control rents, at least for housing benefit tenants, by reducing the level of rent eligible to be counted for housing benefit to those of the cheapest 30% in any area: an attempt to prevent landlords gaming the housing benefit system by raising rents. While this might help to keep rents down for these tenants (although it is likely to mean that benefit claimants will increasingly only be able to access the least desirable housing), there is little evidence of any effect on other rents, so wider rent controls are frequently suggested. But rent controls, unless they are very carefully formulated, will choke off the desired increase in the supply of private rental property. Elsewhere in the EU, controls have not stifled supply, but this is because the

Myth 3 **Leaving owner-occupied housing costs out of the inflation target helped bring about the financial crisis**

It is arguable that the Bank of England's Monetary Policy Committee (of which I was then a member) kept the bank rate too low in the period leading up to the financial crisis. But this was because we failed to pay enough attention to wider financial imbalances and their long-term implications. House prices are not the right indicator of people's housing costs in an inflation measure, as the UK's Consumer Price Advisory Committee has recently concluded. Their preferred approach to measuring owner-occupation costs is based on 'rental equivalence'.[7] This is a measure designed to answer the question: what would the house that I presently occupy cost to rent?

The rationale for this is that house-price rises are only inflation for those contemplating house purchase. Existing homeowners will tend to feel better off, not worse off, when prices go up. If the consumer price index had included housing costs measured in this way in the run-up to the crisis, it would have made little difference to the inflation rate because rents (at least as they were then measured) were not rising particularly quickly. The debate about whether to include housing costs in the consumer price index has been a lively one, but this would not have altered the Monetary Policy Committee's interest rate decisions in the mid 2000s.

There are caveats, however, about the rental equivalence approach to measuring housing costs. In the long term there is a strong relationship between rents and owner-occupation housing costs, but short-term imperfections in the credit market and/or periods of irrational expectations about house prices mean that they can get out of kilter with each other.

controls often fail to keep rents much below market levels. A concerted resort to rent control, then, would simply be an attempt to fight the market by reducing the price of something that other policies have rendered in short supply. It is unlikely to succeed. Changes to encourage longer secure tenancies, or to control rent increases, might achieve a better balance between protecting tenants and retaining an adequate incentive for landlords.

Myth 4 **London and the South East are too congested, so we need to build more houses in the North and fewer in the South East**

It is sometimes argued that people need to move to where the housing is, but it makes much more sense for housing to be built where people want to live and work. If governments really want to tilt the economic geography of the UK from south to north, then improved skills and transport links, the movement of government offices out of London and the creation of new cultural centres all need to come before building new housing. Most experts argue that housing supply should be focused on urban labour markets. Alain Bertaud has pointed out that once cities are thought of in this way, transport issues come to the fore.[8] The alternative – restricting housing development in exactly the places where people want to live, and where settling would improve their welfare – is perverse.

Regional policy (and its costs and benefits) is a vast topic and it cannot be tackled here,[9] but the balance of evidence suggests that, despite considerable expenditure, little success has come from efforts to regenerate declining cities.

It is also unfortunate that better data on rents in the UK is not available. The Office for National Statistics has introduced a recently developed rental series into a new measure of inflation, but at the time of writing this series was being reviewed. Rental data is important for measuring inflation, and for indicating the trend in housing affordability.

Homes where people want to live

At any time different towns and regions will experience very different housing pressures. During the recovery from the financial crisis, London's international status has driven up house prices there. But cities such as Stoke-on-Trent, where the housing market was still being regenerated in the late 2000s, have seen a far slower return to upward price pressure.

Spatial policy has recently moved backwards. In 2010, the coalition government ended regional planning, choosing instead to focus on local planning (through 'local enterprise partnerships'), making it difficult to develop a coherent approach to regional spatial questions. This is a pity both from a development point of view and from an environmental one. Issues of water scarcity, or of biodiversity, are often best considered over quite wide geographical areas, and these debates cannot now easily take place.[10]

Summary

All governments surely want to see the population decently housed, and yet major housing issues are still not being tackled in a systematic way. Politicians find it hard to resist introducing short-term policies that seem to support the popular desire for home ownership, directing subsidy towards those who are nearly able to afford to buy a house, but this is not the best use of taxpayers' money in the housing market.

Economists tend to prefer policies that level the playing field between home ownership and renting, but they are not easy to implement. Policy towards the private rented sector is itself confused: it aims to limit rent rises *and* to encourage more investment, but these are conflicting aims.

The fundamental issue is that a house is inevitably both an investment asset and a provider of housing services. If declining supply relative to demand is likely to result in a long-term trend of rising prices, it will be a major incentive for buying a home.

The UK has experienced a long-run undersupply of housing relative to demand, which rises because of higher incomes and a growing population. (Demand is not the same as 'need': the latter would imply we all lived in houses that just met government-determined space and bedroom allowances.) The recent financial crisis has been followed by a sharp fall in supply, but the shake-out of smaller developers and the loss of construction skills means that just getting back to the level of new housing supply delivered in the mid 2000s may take several more years.

On top of this, foreign buying is distorting the market in key cities (especially London), the tax system could be better structured to encourage housing supply, and there is a basic question as to how much housing is compatible with environmental concerns: both for the UK as a whole and for particular areas.

All these complex and interrelated questions need to be viewed through a clearer policy lens. The rest of this book seeks to do just that, focusing chiefly on private housing. Social housing deserves its own book.

Chapter 2

Post-war planning and housing policy

Successive governments have wanted to ensure that all households have a dwelling of a decent standard and, through good planning, that these homes are in pleasant places. Unfortunately, the objectives of those devising and implementing planning regulations have not always been the same as the objectives of those concerned about housing market outcomes, and this has often resulted in frustration between different arms of government at both national and local levels.

This is not the story of planning in the UK as a whole: policies in Scotland and Northern Ireland (and in Wales since 1998) have increasingly diverged from those in England as a result of devolution. This means that much of the following discussion is about England (although some of the quoted figures are UK-wide ones). Devolving planning complicates policy, since some measures (particularly taxes) have remained national and can rub up against the devolved administrations' housing and planning policies.

A little history helps in understanding today's housing situation, so I give a brief description below of the key planning acts and other regulations, the major changes in the taxation of development and housing, and the shifts in policy towards social and other 'affordable' housing. By detailing some of the relevant history, I give examples of how successive policies have often had unintended consequences because of a failure to anticipate how the market would respond and/or because the impact of economic and credit cycles has been ignored.

The 1950s and 1960s: post-war reconstruction[11]

The most important year in our planning history is 1947, when the Town and Country Planning Act effectively nationalized development rights in England and Wales.[12] From that time on, most developments of any size have required an application for planning permission. This Act also introduced the plan-led system, meaning that decisions on planning applications needed to be made in accordance with the local plan unless there were specific reasons not to do so (these are called material considerations, an example being a shortage of school places). Despite many modifications, in principle these two key features still hold sway in England.

The concept of the green belt was also formalized in 1947 as a means to contain urban sprawl. Only London had a green belt initially, but in 1955 Duncan Sandys, then minister for housing, encouraged all local authorities to establish their own green belts.

At first this regime was positive for new housing supply. During the 1950s and 1960s the number of dwellings completed each year in the UK reached a historically high level, peaking at 426,000 in 1968. Local authorities were building on a very large scale for social renting, and there was also a growing supply from housing associations. Social rent completions in the UK averaged over 190,000 per year in the 1950s, and over 160,000 in the 1960s. Private completions rose from just

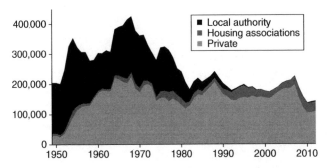

Figure 2.1. UK housing completions. *Source*: Department for Communities and Local Government.

90,000 a year in the 1950s to almost 200,000 in the 1960s.[13] But demolition of unfit housing was also taking place, so overall figures for additions to the stock were less impressive: while total completions ran at around 280,000 in the 1950s, the stock rose by only 250,000 annually; in the 1960s, completions averaged about 360,000 but the annual increase in stock averaged just 263,000.

Nevertheless, the annual increases in the number of homes were far greater than they have been in the most recent two decades. In the 1990s fewer than 35,000 social rental homes were built annually, and in the 2000s this dropped below 25,000 before picking up to over 30,000 again by the end of the decade. Private completions averaged 156,000 in the 1990s and 167,000 in the 2000s (see figure 2.1). For England alone in the 2000s, social housing averaged 19,000 completions and private housing 128,000.

The high rate of home building during the 1950s and, especially, the 1960s suggests that there is nothing about nationalized development rights and a plan-led system that intrinsically inhibits residential development. Active public policy played a large role: fourteen new towns were designated in the UK in the 1960s in response to faster projected population growth (this projection was later revised down sharply, bringing about a reduction in the new towns programme). However, subsequent changes in planning regulation, the funding of subsidized housing, and attitudes to development and the development industry have all combined to reduce the rate at which homes have been added to the stock in the face of rising demand.

The 1970s, 1980s and 1990s: planning comes under pressure

The early success in boosting housing supply concealed underlying problems. Under the 1947 Act, local authorities were primarily responsible for drawing up local plans, which then required ministerial approval. This proved unwieldy, with long delays in amending plans to take account of the rapidly changing economic and demographic pressures of the 1960s. In 1968 a two-tier system was introduced, with counties responsible for 'structure plans' taking a more strategic view. Until 1992 these were subject to approval by the secretary of state.

This change did little to help. It took until 1975 for the first structure plan to be approved, and plans were often so long in preparation that they were out of date by the time they were adopted. During the 1980s, structure plans were much criticised for increasing uncertainty. The Planning and Compensation Act of 1991 aimed to tackle this. It enhanced the plan-led system by giving the plan *primacy* in development control; it made district-wide local plans mandatory; it removed the requirement for central government approval of structure plans; and it abandoned small-area local plans. Despite this apparent tidying up, the planning system continued to be criticized for causing delays, because of the lack of coordination between different levels of government, and because of generally excessive bureaucracy. It is often argued that the stronger role given to local plans *increased* the difficulty of gaining planning permission, rather than making it easier.

The 2000s: an accelerating pace of change

The Planning and Compensation Act of 2004 abolished structure plans, introducing a bigger role for Regional Spatial Strategies to be approved by the secretary of state, alongside a 'portfolio of local plans' developed at district level. It was perhaps curious that a review was ordered into land-use planning at the end of 2005, very soon after the 2004 Act: a review that I was asked to lead. The government of the day realized that there was continued impatience with the planning system, particularly when it came to large infrastructure projects. Besides, it already seemed like the process for producing the new local development plans was (yet again) unduly cumbersome.

Following my review, the Planning Act 2008 introduced a new planning process for major infrastructure. For housing, the key measure was the concept of the Community Infrastructure Levy, which I discuss in chapter 7. Also, the processes for local plan production were streamlined.

Since 2010 the coalition government has continued to reform the planning system. Their initial rhetoric was about localism and greater democracy, reflected in the 2011 Localism Act, which abolished the regional tier of planning. Among other changes, this Act introduced a 'duty to cooperate': a not very successful attempt to ensure that local authorities worked together on planning matters of joint concern (such as transport projects that straddle local boundaries).

Fears from the pro-development lobby that these changes would stifle development quickly gave way to a wave of concern from environmental groups during consultation on the new National Planning Policy Framework. This relatively short document (which did not require primary legislation) came into effect in March 2012, replacing many pages of planning guidance with a shorter and less complex framework. The main sources of contention were as follows.

- The strong emphasis on planning for growth, which led to concerns about environmental sustainability.
- The introduction of a presumption in favour of development where there is no existing plan.

Local authorities were given a year to put plans in place, but in spring 2013 a substantial minority of councils had not even submitted plans for approval by the planning inspectorate, which potentially left them vulnerable to speculative planning applications.

Hard on the heels of the Localism Act, the Growth and Infrastructure Bill included still more changes: a planning authority judged to be performing badly could now be 'designated' for a period, and during that time applications in that area would have to be made to the secretary of state directly.

The impact of legislative change

The post-war period has therefore been characterized by lots of legislative change designed to drive or influence behaviour at local level towards the current goals of central government. A persistent frustration has been the tardiness of many local authorities in putting in place plans that conform to the latest national strategy. But it might equally be argued that the ability to develop plans was hindered by the frequency of changes in the regime under which they were to be prepared. There is often a significant gap between national policy and the inevitable wrangles and compromises at local level in establishing plans and delivering development control decisions. In influencing local authorities, the detail of planning legislation may be less important than the overall policy context that central government communicates.

Development taxation

As well as the various planning acts discussed above, the past sixty years have also seen a variety of attempts to tax development gains: the increase in land values that often results from the granting of planning permission. The 1947 Act provided £300 million for compensating landowners whose development rights had been restricted. It also introduced a 100% Development Land Tax, on the basis that more land would come to market if there were no hope of gain from land hoarding. Unfortunately, landowners instead came to hope for a change of government, to a regime that would reduce this tax, and in 1954 the tax was indeed repealed and the compensation scheme suspended.

Subsequent attempts to capture part of the land value gains from planning permission were made in 1967, 1974 and 1985. All raised less revenue than expected, and all resulted in land being held off the market in the hope of a more favourable taxation regime. Since the 1970s the main way in which value has been extracted from development for the public purse has been through planning *agreements*, which can range from restrictions on the use of a site to charges for infrastructure and facilities related to the development. Their legitimacy and precise scope have been the source of much controversy, with periodic government circulars issued to extend or restrict this scope. Changes since 1991, when planning *obligations* were introduced, are covered in chapter 7.

Housing policy and planning

Legislative changes reveal shifts in policy emphasis. In the 1950s and 1960s the focus was on reconstruction and improvement of the council housing stock (although today we look on the surviving tower blocks from that period with little enthusiasm). In the 1970s, economic volatility and increasing pressure on public spending, together with reduced demolition of older housing, resulted in a slower rate of new building of public sector housing, although private sector building continued at much the same pace.

The 1980s was a period of economic deregulation, both in the mortgage market and when it came to private rentals. The Housing Act 1980 introduced Right to Buy for council tenants as a major policy; this resulted in a rise in owner-occupation, a fall in social housing stock and an increased marginalization of social housing tenants as better-off people became homeowners.

During the 1980s and 1990s increased demographic pressure, especially in the South East, collided with rising concerns about the environment, limiting the land available for housing. Private sector housebuilding was not able to compensate for the slower rate of construction by local authorities and housing associations. Despite increasing concern about the inadequacy of new supply, planning policy guidance on housing became more restrictive, with Planning Policy Guidance 3: Housing representing the high point of this trend. Issued in

2000, this stressed higher density (more homes per hectare), greater use of brownfield land and urban redevelopment. In the wake of the 2004 Housing Supply Review, a revised document, Planning Policy Statement 3, was produced in 2006. It sought to make housing supply more responsive to market signals. Housing supply did pick up around this time but then fell back very sharply as a result of the financial crisis that started in 2007. Little recovery in new supply was apparent until the introduction in spring 2013 of a government scheme (Help to Buy) to support mortgages on new-build homes.

There is much evidence of local resistance to a higher rate of housebuilding, especially in the South East. A recent study by Savills estate agents suggests that many local authorities in the South East continue to have plans that do not meet predicted demand[14] – and even then, the inadequate plans that are in place may be difficult to deliver because of local campaigns against housing development that sway councillors' decisions. Local resentment has in some places been fuelled by the fact that developers have for a time been able to gain permissions more easily where there is no local plan in place.

It is sometimes argued that resistance to development would be lower if new housing were better designed, including using custom build or self-build as well as developers' standard products. But while good design of dwellings is important, it will not outweigh worries about congestion, changes in the character of a locality or a decrease in house prices.

Summary

The history of planning policy reveals two persistent failures. First, the frequent attempts to improve the system, such as the move to a plan-led process in 1991, have in practice all too often added complications, increased delay and provided more scope for opposition to development. Second, attempts to tax development land have often restricted land supply.

In 2005 a government-commissioned major evaluation of housing policy concluded that

> the housing system as a whole has *not* become more robust, responsive and self-sustaining. This has left a legacy of massively different outcomes between those who are already reasonably housed and those trying to gain access to the system.[15]

This conclusion still stands in 2014.

Chapter 3

Economic sense and planning

What explains the history of disappointment from planning policy? And why should there be a conflict between economics and planning?

Economics, properly understood, is a set of useful tools that should help planners think about their problems. Equally, economists should not cavil at planning, which aims to tackle the familiar economic problem of 'externalities'[16] and, more ambitiously, to develop places that are pleasant to live in and function well for business. Yet the often vitriolic debate in 2011–12 around the introduction of the National Planning Policy Framework (NPPF) pitched planning against economics, as the following quote from Friends of the Earth demonstrates.

> Friends of the Earth is concerned that the draft NPPF has been used to set out a deregulatory approach as part of a package of planning reform designed to prioritise private business interests in the name of economic growth. Friends of the Earth believes that the planning system is an essential public function that must continue to deliver decision-making in the public interest.[17]

I came fresh to the planning system in 2003 when I was asked to undertake a review of housing supply for the government. Reading the planning guidance that was applicable to housing at that time ('PPG3'), I was surprised by the strong emphasis that was placed on achieving higher densities for residential development, on using previously developed (brownfield) sites first, and on restricting car parking. In many places such policies would make sense, but PPG3 had no clear justification for their wide application, and barely acknowledged possible negative consequences.

The omissions were also striking. The indicators that local authorities were supposed to track were, by and large, simply a list of whether or not the plans were being achieved. If the success of planning is to be judged simply in terms of fulfilling plans – without looking at wider indicators (most obviously, house prices) to judge if the plans were appropriate – then this is just a self-referential activity of limited value.

Surely planning could be better?

What is the purpose of planning?

The earliest planning regulations stemmed from concerns over public health sparked by the poor living conditions in industrializing urban areas in the nineteenth century. The main objective was summed up in 1947 as 'to regulate the development and use of land in the public interest', and in 2004 as 'to contribute to the achievement of sustainable development'.[18] Planning theory often reflects prevailing political trends[19] and it is not an economics-free zone. Welfare economics underlies much of the work on urban structure and most planners are fully engaged with considering how to enable their local economies to develop successfully. The tendency for planners to think they know best, however, is long established. In 1941 Harrisson[20] commented that he had 'never met any group of people who "scratched each others' backs" more than planners did'.

However, by the early 2000s much planning *policy* (to be distinguished from the *planners* who enact it) had drifted away from the underlying economic forces. There was a lack of interest in price changes as an indication of demand in an area (except that very low prices in deprived areas were recognized as a signal of distress). There was a view that housebuilders were doing something undesirable in wanting to build three- and four-bedroom detached houses because these were the most profitable, whereas an economist might argue that this was an appropriate response to the relative price of space in smaller versus larger dwellings. Officials believed that as new households were smaller, new housing units should be smaller too. One outcome of this view and the focus on increasing density is that new stock in England is smaller, on average, than that being built in most other EU countries.

This mindset led to the perception of widespread market failure and a rather self-righteous view of planning. People opposed to aspects of planning policy were characterized as lacking concern for non-monetary values or being indifferent to the environment. There was little interest in the possibility of either unintended consequences from planning policies or administrative failure.

It would be a very radical market economist indeed who argued that development should *only* respond to price signals, and that planning should play no role. Environmental concerns, the costs of providing infrastructure to different locations, spillover effects of bad-neighbour factors such as noise, the importance of well-designed buildings, and social considerations are all perfectly good reasons to lean against, or even reject, pure market signals. But this needs to be done with proper consideration of the costs and benefits.

No sensible person would wish to abandon planning. The NPPF started with a blank sheet of paper and yet retained, to some degree, concerns about town centres, density of development, mixed communities, best use of transport facilities and many other aspects of the previous planning guidance. But equally, no sensible person should want to ignore the economic issues.

Planning and housing policy

Planning is vital for a local authority in identifying better and worse places to locate new housing, and in assessing details such as the design and layout of sites, but local policymakers find it hard to answer the question: how much development is the right amount? Before the introduction of PPG3 in 2000, household projections usually formed the basis for answering this question, but this approach was not uncontested.

A key example of the housing numbers problem came at the end of the 1990s. The local authorities in the south east of England (excluding London) proposed a target of building 33,000 houses per year in their region for the next twenty years. The report from the Examination in Public of the South East Plan, chaired by Professor Stephen Crow, recommended that this target should be increased to 55,000 houses per year. The then deputy prime minister, John Prescott, set out an annual target of 43,000. He said that the panel had used, 'a rigid "predict and provide" approach' and had failed to pay enough attention to sustainability. His comment encapsulates enduring features of the debate around housing, especially in the South East.

Subsequently, PPG3 included a shift from 'predict and provide' to 'plan, monitor, manage'. What is the difference?

Rather than predicting the number of households likely to form in the South East, the starting point became the Regional Planning Guidance number. This was approved by government as a balance, struck in an opaque manner, between unconstrained household projections and sustainability factors. The monitoring was then largely about seeing whether the plan was being carried out and adjusting future intentions ('managing') if actual housing supply numbers turned out to be too low, or indeed too high, *relative to that plan*.

What might a good methodology look like, and how would it differ from what is happening now?

A good starting point is to define success. Many people would agree with the general proposition that everyone should have access to a decent home at a price they can afford. But that leaves plenty of room for debate, not just about subsidies for those unlikely to be able to afford housing but also about how far demand, rather than need, should be accommodated. The distinction here is that a couple might be thought to 'need' at most a two-bedroom house – but they might want and be able to afford ('demand') three bedrooms. Questioning whether to meet demand is only relevant if there is some sound reason for limiting the supply of housing: in terms of dwelling units, in terms of space per person, or in terms of particular locations. Otherwise, we would allow supply to respond freely to demand: by designating land that was *not* to be developed and then allowing planning permissions to be granted anywhere else, for example. And while demand is driven in part by population, fundamentally it is rising incomes that boost demand for space. To focus only on population is to miss a large part of the point – and in any case, population projections are not reliable.

Projections produced by the Office for National Statistics (ONS) set out, on the basis of past behaviour and demographic

Table 3.1. Recent thirty-year household formation projections (annual average growth in thousands).

	2004 based	2006 based	2008 based
North West	26	27	22
West Midlands	19	21	18
London	39	34	36
South East	35	39	40
England	**223**	**252**	**234**

Source: Office for National Statistics.
England projection for 2011: 221,000.

trends, how many households will wish to form. The history of post-war *population* projections indicates that they often turn out to be wrong. Birth rates, mortality and (recently) migration trends are all subject to considerable uncertainty. Looking at the ONS projections for household formation in England over successive overlapping thirty-year periods, they have fluctuated markedly, and even more so if considered at a regional level (see Table 3.1[21]). Wisely, the ONS publish wide ranges around their central projections, with migration trends a particular uncertainty.

The number of households that have actually formed, for a given population, has in recent years tended to be lower than the ONS projections. In the 2001–6 period, it is estimated (there is uncertainty around all these numbers) that household formation in England was 17% lower than the ONS had predicted, with only 168,000 households being formed annually: a difference of 34,000 households per year. In the North East, household formation was 41% lower than the projections, and in the West Midlands 28%. The ONS's over-prediction was much less marked for London, the South East and the South West.[22]

> **Myth 5** **There are plenty of houses, we just need to occupy the empty homes and share homes more fairly**
>
> In 2013 there were 635,000 empty homes in England according to the Empty Homes Agency. But some level of vacancy is to be expected. For example, many are empty after someone's death while probate is being obtained. It is right to seek to reduce the number of long-term empty homes (those unoccupied for more than six months) but there are now only around 230,000 of these.
>
> It is also true that many owner-occupied homes are under-occupied. And it may be that some elderly people could be encouraged to move into smaller properties with support, if the right kind of home were available. But many households will prefer to have spare rooms, and more of us now use a room at home as an office.

The most plausible explanation for this might be that the tendency for people to move south was underestimated, but a shortage of housing and rising prices in the south have meant more sharing. Evidence that housing supply has been insufficient is seen in the increase in young adults living at home, estimated by the ONS to be rising by around 40,000 a year. Overcrowding has been on an upward trend over the past decade, especially in the private rented sector.

Five-year land supply

Population projections may, then, be a starting point for plans, but they should not be the whole story. Under the new planning regime, local authorities are charged with ensuring that they have identified a *deliverable* five-year land supply for housing. How should they estimate how much land this requires?

The latest guidance proposes a number of indicators.[23] In the subsidized sector: social housing waiting lists and rents paid by those on housing benefits. In the market sector: market rents. For owner-occupied housing: the general rate of increase in house prices, and the level of prices relative to local incomes – especially the ratio of mortgage payments to income levels for aspiring first-time buyers. Taken together, these could indicate a developing imbalance between supply and demand (not need) in the market, or in part of it. It is very welcome that the recent, much improved and simplified, policy guidance stresses monitoring these market indicators. Rising prices will reflect financial market changes as well as demand and supply imbalances, and these can be hard to distinguish. But to the extent that demand is not being met, this imposes a cost on households as prices rise. And the costs may run wider, as others have argued, if planning prevents cities from growing and achieving the full benefits of agglomeration of economic activities.[24]

Less helpfully, local authorities can attempt to second-guess developers about what type of houses should be built. Apart from ensuring provision for the elderly and disabled, it is unclear that this intervention with the market is justified.

As explained earlier, the NPPF created a strong incentive for planning authorities to put plans in place. But this takes time. A quick look at the Planning Inspectorate website suggests that it takes at least a year from the submission of a 'core strategy' (the basic development guidance for a local authority) through to approval and adoption, and this can be much longer if the planning inspector does not consider the submission likely to be 'sound' (at present this means in con-formity with the NPPF).

Some proposed plans have been judged 'unsound'. For ex-ample, the examination of the Bath and North Somerset core strategy was suspended in mid 2012 because (among other reasons) the inspector considered the methodology used to project future housing need was inadequate. It is clear that the Planning Inspectorate's role is vital to ensure that over-all the individual plans add up to an adequate supply. But the planning inspectors are unelected, they cannot substitute for proper cooperation on housing across local authority bound-aries, and they can be resented for forcing central govern-ment policy on local areas.

The issue of sustainability

Many objections to planning applications are made on the grounds that the proposed housing location is 'unsustain-able'. The definition of sustainability was a major point of contention around the NPPF. The final version referred to the United Nations definition: 'meeting the needs of the present without compromising the ability of future generations to meet their own needs'. It is not easy to turn this into a useful guide, and arguably the NPPF does not fully clarify the con-cept. However, in broad terms the ideal is a planning system that supports economic development and our well-being today without compromising the future environment.

Discussions of sustainability therefore involve interlocked questions of economic development, land-use, density, social considerations (what makes a 'place'), transport, water sup-ply and biodiversity. At a high level, the debate could be char-acterized by two conflicting views.

Those who are generally 'anti-development' argue that the density of population across London and the South East is too high, leading to undue stress on water, on biodiversity and on people, due to congested travel conditions (including concerns about car usage and air quality). Where housing is built it should be dense in terms of dwellings per hectare, and brownfield sites should be developed ahead of greenfield ones.

The alternative view is that with good planning and better infrastructure we could meet the rising demand for housing in the South East, and that while high density may be appropriate in some places, we need to be concerned about liveability and people's access to green space. Some greenfield sites will therefore have to be developed if we are to meet demand. This view also tends to stress the importance of gardens rather than farmland in supporting biodiversity.

There are of course commonalities, such as concern about climate change (both reducing carbon emissions and developing a built environment that is more resilient to the impacts of climate change, such as flooding), and both groups care about biodiversity and the preservation of significant landscapes.

Is London and the South East, or England as a whole, overcrowded?

England is a relatively densely populated country, with 411 people per square kilometre. In the EU, only the Netherlands, at 496 people per square kilometre, is more densely populated. The overall figure conceals wide variation, though: there are 14,203 people per square kilometre in Islington but just 46 in West Devon. And it is worth bearing in mind that it is not just the South East that has high population density. Of course, London has a high density – 5,285 people per square kilometre (though some major global cities are much more dense) – and even taken together, London and the South East have a population density of 825. But at 502 people per square kilometre, the North West is more dense than Eastern England (at 309). All this regional data hides large underlying variation at local authority level, but the big point is that it is rather more complex than North versus South.

Is there a strong environmental reason for constraining the rate of household formation or for limiting the amount of space per house relative to demand? Put another way, is it a good thing if rises in the price of land for housing exceed the rate of growth of incomes, so that space within dwelling units (and for gardens) becomes more expensive relative to household budgets?

As argued above, housing is income elastic: as people get better off they would like to consume more private space, and this seems to be particularly true in the UK, as brought out in the recent OBR work on house prices.[25] If supply fails to respond to rising demand, the inevitable consequence will be rising prices and problems of affordability for people on the margins of home ownership. To strike the right balance between meeting unconstrained demand and managing supply we need a clear view of the right environmental price.

In many places there is an obvious answer. Areas of Outstanding Natural Beauty, the National Parks, public parks, village greens, Sites of Special Scientific Interest and the like are all subject to stringent planning restrictions, implying that the social and/or environmental value of keeping this land open is high – in some cases almost infinite. These areas are very large: Sites of Special Scientific Interest cover 8.2% of England, Areas of Outstanding Natural Beauty 15.6% and National Parks 7.6%. There are further EU designations that protect over 11%.

Myth 6 **We are running out of land and there is a danger of 'concreting over' the South East**

Currently in England around 10.6% of land is built-up, and this includes gardens and parks. As Paul Cheshire has argued, there is a danger that green belts mainly benefit the house prices of those already living within them.[26] Green belt is often land of poor quality that fails to deliver access to open space, as was once intended.

While many of these areas overlap, up to 25% of England is probably protected in some way.[27]

The other big protected area is the green belt. While this is often misunderstood to be an environmental designation, its purpose is in fact to support planning goals such as containing urban sprawl and ensuring separation between distinct communities. It covers a much larger area than the name suggests: in 2012/13 around 13% of England was green belt. Proposals to alter the green belt often provoke emotional reactions, even though it would seem reasonable that planning or even environmental considerations might suggest that green belt revisions would be justified over time. Unfortunately, in the Planning Policy Guidance published in March 2014, the protection of green belt land from housing development was effectively tightened. The guidance now states that 'unmet housing need…is unlikely to outweigh the harm to the green belt'.

In 2005 the Office of the Deputy Prime Minister commissioned a study into the sustainability of different rates of new housing supply and different geographic distributions.[28] This was in response to my government-commissioned Review of Housing Supply,[29] which suggested that further work was needed to understand the trade-off between the benefits of meeting unconstrained demand for housing and the environmental costs. The 2005 analysis looked at the impacts on land-use, CO_2 emissions, additional waste and additional water. Importantly, it distinguished between the impact of additional population and the impact of housing this population more generously in terms of numbers of dwellings and space. The government concluded from this work that the environmental impacts were not severe enough to rule out more house-building, but disappointingly it made no real attempt to evaluate exactly what trade-off might be appropriate.[30]

A thorough review of these issues then appeared in 2010 in the Land Use Futures project for the government-sponsored Foresight series,[31] with the following suggestions being made.

- Decisions on land use need to be taken in a 'more coherent and integrated way', not just between different spatial levels of government but also between the various sectoral bodies, so that issues such as climate change, biodiversity, transport, energy, etc., are properly reflected.[32]
- Land values need to recognize psychological costs. The cost of having a new development on your doorstep is not just the economic one of a lower home value but also unease about places changing and about loss of local landscape. Of course, these concerns need to be set against the potentially larger benefit for those gaining access to new housing, but proper consideration of these non-financial costs, hard as they are to evaluate, should be taken into account when deciding where to locate new developments.
- Better-aligned incentives (so that communities see financial benefits as well as costs in accepting new housing) would help resolve the dilemmas (this is discussed further in chapters 6 and 7).

Despite all this work, there is still little coherent discussion about whether residential land prices in places where there is most pressure for additional housing (largely but not only London and the South East) match or exceed the full costs of housing development. These should include both environmental costs and social costs such as congestion. Nor is there much in-depth analysis of the costs and benefits that might accrue to any serious attempt to shift economic activity around the country.[33]

Density at site level

Those wanting to prevent extensive development on open land argue for high densities on already-developed land, claiming that this also helps to reduce travel, cutting carbon emissions. While the evidence for this is mixed, it is certainly true that a large high-density city will only be able to function economically if it has good public transport, and this also keeps carbon emissions down. But dense cities can raise other problems: heat in summer, for example. And many people prefer a more rural or small-town lifestyle, or different settings at different times of life. This suggests that a mix of densities and types of development will best meet demand and these wider considerations.

A planning misconception

Sometimes planners seem to regard higher property values as a good outcome. Indeed, one of many difficulties in making judgements on planning decisions is how to distinguish the 'good' price increases of a more successful place from the 'bad' ones reflecting unduly constrained land supply.

It is a difficult evaluation. After all, UK housing market models suggest that big supply changes lead to only small changes in affordability, at least in the medium term.[34] In the short term at the local scale this effect is hard to discern. But in the long term many households nationally would benefit from a gradual improvement in the affordability of living space.

Administrative costs of planning

The activity of planning is itself costly, although it is vital to distinguish the costs that bring valuable benefits (for example, the costs of public consultation, or of getting the details of design right). Other costs – especially administrative delay, or demands for detailed information that is not really useful in evaluating an application – are clearly wasteful. A recent report concluded that the performance of local authorities in handling planning applications was still very variable, and it also found evidence of delays in responses from other agencies, such as the Highways Agency or the Environment Agency.[35] In 2010 Adrian Penfold produced a set of recommendations on how to resolve the delays around non-planning consents[36] (often issues around highways or the environment), but these consents still often hold up development that has planning permission. In 2014 the government launched a consultation aimed at cutting the time for these other consents to eight weeks.

Many have argued that, while these other agencies should meet deadlines, crude timescales for local authority decisions on planning applications are not that helpful.[29,35] A more nuanced approach to performance is needed. Despite this, in 2014 the government was still attempting to put pressure on local authorities to take planning decisions more quickly.

Development control (giving permission to particular proposals) might also be made easier if local plans were more rule-based, so that once the plan existed it was clearer and simpler for proposals in line with the plan to obtain permission. This kind of zoning exists in other countries and has often been suggested here – to replace a system in which we argue not only about the plans but also, subsequently, about all the individual developments.

Summary

There should be no quarrel between planners and economists, but planners need to recognize that their activities impose costs as well as bringing benefits, and that these costs are often hidden. The big cost is that restricting supply increases house prices. Success is often judged by whether the plan is fulfilled, rather than by looking at wider outcomes. Planning frequently attempts to tackle environmental issues by resisting people's preferences for where they want to live and the density at which they want to live. It is not easy to assess whether any plan is 'right' in this respect – especially when it comes to the trade-off in London and the South East between environmental and social constraints and housing – but the government ought to address this. At present the Planning Inspectorate is implicitly being asked to tackle these questions as they perform the difficult but vital job of assessing the adequacy of housing provision in local plans.

However, working at the local level the large regional disparities in the level of prices that make it hard for people to move around the country cannot be addressed. London's high prices are perhaps a special case. In other countries the price level in the capital has moved away from elsewhere, reflecting the role of global, rather than domestic, wealth.

The recent introduction of the NPPF and the new simplified guidance have improved the approach to planning for housing. The guidance discourages local authorities from undertaking expensive consultancy studies and wasteful surveys to assess future need, and encourages using market signals to assess demand. However, further changes to the development process are needed – some administrative (especially around non-planning consents) and others more far reaching. While not wanting to return to the previous regional planning system, some stronger direction for planning across local authority boundaries is needed. The cost of keeping land open, including the green belt, relative to the benefit of meeting demand needs to be more explicit, and a rule-based approach to permissions would improve certainty in development. Radical changes to planning to be more pro-development everywhere would risk hardening local opposition to planning applications. But we will need some central direction to get the new towns and major urban extensions that are needed.

Economists (including me) may also need to be less dogmatic. We should recognize that people will value the special features of a place, and we should consider the psychological effects of additional development. Financial values are not the only values that matter. Planning decisions will therefore always be a matter of balancing these factors, but the important point is that all the relevant factors need to be in the mix.

Chapter 4

Does the UK housing market make the economy unstable?

In June 2003 the big issue was whether or not the UK should join the euro. Gordon Brown had devised five tests to judge this question, and on the basis of the Treasury's analysis he announced that the answer was no. A key part of that analysis was that the UK's housing market was more volatile than in other major EU countries, resulting in greater volatility of household spending and, therefore, of the whole economy.

Both the Barker review of housing supply and the Miles review of the UK mortgage market were set up in part to consider how the UK housing market could be reformed to reduce this volatility.[37] The UK housing market does indeed have some idiosyncratic features, and the recent eurozone crisis has given ample demonstration of how collapsing housing markets (obvious examples being those in Spain and the Republic of Ireland) exacerbate economic difficulties. This chapter considers the relationship between the housing market and the wider economy, casts some doubt on the solutions sought by the government in 2003, and comments on how the new structure of financial market regulation will affect the housing market.

Housing supply and house price volatility

The previous chapter discussed how undersupply has contributed to a long-term problem of housing affordability. In 2003 there was particular concern because, while house prices had been increasing quite rapidly since 1997, the rate of new supply in England had fallen to its lowest level since 1947. But how far a supply response is the right answer to rising prices depends on the reason for those price rises. To the extent that higher prices reflect looser credit conditions, this is a short-term trend that rising supply should not be expected to offset. After all, each year new supply is less than 1% of the stock.

The key argument in my housing supply review rested much more on long-term trends in house prices relative to earnings (although it is often misrepresented as an attempt to boost supply in response to mortgage market changes). Real house prices in the UK had risen more than in almost all other major EU economies over the thirty years to 2001. Much economic evidence suggests that, over the long term, new supply increases less in the UK than it does in these other economies when house prices rise.[38]

It is unlikely that new housing supply could offset large swings in house prices driven by shifts in financial conditions, and it is also undesirable. The experiences of Spain and Ireland illustrate the risks of housebuilding responding too strongly to changes in credit conditions and a house price bubble (which means house prices today are influenced by unrealistic expectations of tomorrow's prices). But it is notable that new supply adjusts far more readily when credit conditions tighten than when they ease. Housing completions in England dropped from a peak of around 177,000 per year in 2007 to under 110,000 in 2010: a reduction of almost 40%. Even this collapse in new supply is unlikely to have made more than a small contribution to arresting the decline in house prices during the financial crisis of 2007–9. The dramatic cuts in interest rates, along with quantitative easing and government action on mortgage rescue and forbearance by lenders, did rather more to stabilize prices.

The long-term failure of housing supply to match demand can, however, exacerbate volatility when prices are rising. It means that housing becomes continually more expensive relative to incomes. This intensifies a desire to 'get on the housing ladder' early, as the only way to protect effectively against future house price rises, fuelling a tendency for housing market bubbles.

Long-term mortgages

Back in 2003 the Treasury argued that the UK had a stronger link between house prices and household consumption than most euro area countries. It suggested that this could be explained by the UK's relatively high level of mortgage debt compared with household income, combined with the prevalence of mortgage loans on variable interest rates.

The Miles review attributed the dominance of variable mortgage interest rates to a number of factors. The main ones were borrowers having a poor understanding of interest rate risk, the limited portability of mortgages between lenders, the lack of suitable financing for mortgage lenders, and lenders being unable to charge enough if fixed-rate mortgages were redeemed early. Only some of these issues have been addressed: for example, there have been changes in the regulation of the mortgage sales process to improve borrowers' awareness of the risk to their finances if interest rates rise.

However, the proportion of new mortgages taken out on fixed rates did increase in the years before 2007, with these mortgages accounting for over half of the value of outstanding loans in that year. But the proportion then fell back again, and the fixed-rate share of outstanding mortgages is now 35% (although in 2013 the share of *new* borrowing at fixed rates was over 80%). These fixed rates are not necessarily long term; few are fixed for more than nine years.

A move to more fixed-rate mortgages may be a mixed blessing. There is some merit in having household consumption respond to changes in the short-term interest rate set by the Bank of England. Otherwise, monetary policy would be more reliant on other economic mechanisms, such as changes in the exchange rate or business investment, and it is not clear that this would always improve economic performance.

House prices and household consumption

How much does household spending depend on house prices? In the mid 2000s, some people suggested that the Monetary Policy Committee should do more to dampen house price rises. House prices can affect the growth of the wider economy through two possible channels: as collateral (housing equity can be used as security when borrowing, including borrowing for business purposes) or as wealth (households may spend more if rising house prices make them feel better off). There is good evidence that the collateral channel works, though there is uncertainty about its strength.[39]

The wealth effect is less clear-cut. When house prices rise, households who are finally settled or planning to downsize may feel better off. But those still wishing to join the housing ladder, and those planning to move up it, may feel worse off.[40]

In Monetary Policy Committee meetings at the time I used to joke that every rise in house prices made me feel worse off, as it added to the amount of money I would need to help my sons into home ownership.

In its November 2004 inflation report, the Monetary Policy Committee argued that since around 2001 the correlation between consumer spending and house prices had fallen. The *reason* for an increase in house prices will affect how powerful its impact on consumer spending is. The strong link between house prices and consumer spending during the house price booms in the 1970s and 1980s reflected the fact that households experienced strong income growth during those periods, and were optimistic that this would continue.

By contrast, household income growth was relatively weak during the early–mid 2000s. The house price boom at that time was driven primarily by looser credit conditions: not just lower interest rates, but also more lax lending criteria. The latter included a rising share of self-certification mortgages (where the lender had weak evidence of the borrower's income) and some interest-only mortgages where there was no clear plan for repayment of the capital sum. So while looser credit conditions and the greater stability of the economy (there was an uninterrupted seventeen-year period of gross domestic product (GDP) growth up to the first quarter of 2008) increased households' propensity to borrow, weak real income growth meant no big rise in consumer spending.

Housing's role in the UK financial crisis

The sharp rise in house prices in the run-up to the financial crisis, did not, therefore, foster wider economic volatility through rising consumer spending. Sluggish new supply acted as an underlying factor contributing to unsustainable house price expectations, but in the post-crisis recession, the lack of new building was helpful. Defying many more gloomy forecasts, UK-wide nominal house prices fell by around 20% peak-to-trough, and by the second quarter of 2014 had recovered to stand around 10% below their peak according to the Halifax House Price Index.

Falling residential construction did have an impact, accounting for a 0.7% fall in GDP (the total GDP fall to the low point of the recession was 7.2%).

Will recent policy changes reduce volatility?

Reducing housing market volatility matters not just because it affects the overall economy. Price volatility can mean that households' long-term prospects depend on the point of the cycle at which they first buy a home; and it raises risk, and therefore cost, for those investing in the private rented sector, pushing up rents.[41]

The 2010 coalition government has put in place changes in financial regulation that are intended to limit damaging credit cycles. For the housing market, the significant changes are that the regulation of financial institutions has been moved back to the Bank of England under the Prudential Regulation Authority (PRA); that a new and more robust Financial Conduct Authority now regulates how financial institutions deal with their customers; and that the Bank of England has a new Financial Policy Committee (FPC) to tackle overall financial stability.

It is not yet clear how this new framework will play out, or how these various committees will mesh with each other, with the Monetary Policy Committee and, indeed, with the Treasury and government policy more widely. As the taxpayer ultimately underwrites systemic financial stability, but also wants economic growth, balancing these two aims is perhaps a question for the government rather than for a regulator.[42] Regardless of these more philosophical doubts, in practice the PRA should ensure that mortgage lenders are better capitalized and therefore less prone to the kind of tensions that precipitated the financial crisis, and the Financial Conduct Authority should ensure that mortgage lending is on a more sustainable basis as far the borrower is concerned. The latter was given effect when the Mortgage Market Review provisions were implemented in April 2014.

The FPC has perhaps the most crucial role. Its task is 'macroprudential', meaning that it manages systemic risk across the whole financial system rather than the affairs of individual firms or households. To carry this out, the FPC is able to make recommendations to the PRA and the Financial Conduct Authority, and also give these institutions directions with regard to changing the amount of capital that financial institutions have to hold.[43] This would be one of the tools to hand if the FPC became concerned about a housing 'bubble'. The toolkit has been increased by the proposal that the FPC will be able to make recommendations about maximum loan-to-income ratios. The FPC can also make recommendations about the interest rate stress test used by lenders in affordability assessments (and indeed it did so in June 2014), to reduce the risk of borrowers being unduly vulnerable to a rising rate environment. Deciding there is evidence of a systemic risk from a housing market bubble is a difficult call for the FPC, not least given the regional variations in house price trends. In 2014 the divergence between strong house price inflation in London (fuelled by foreign cash buyers, who will not be affected by mortgage restrictions) and a rather subdued market elsewhere illustrates the uncertainties that policymakers have to consider.

With the benefit of twenty-twenty hindsight, the Monetary Policy Committee failed to give enough consideration to financial imbalances and rising debt levels in the run-up to the financial crisis. Using the bank rate alone to dampen the housing market would have meant big rises in interest rates, damaging the wider economy (although perhaps less damaging than the financial crisis proved). Tackling financial risks directly using one of the tools available to the FPC should prove more effective.

Summary

The arguments about whether the housing market causes wider economic volatility are complex. Short-term swings in the housing market are primarily driven by people's expectations about their incomes and, more importantly, changes in credit conditions. The long-running undersupply of housing can exacerbate upward price movements, but it proved a source of stability when there was a risk of big price falls after the crisis. It is ironic to note that weak supply and the prevalence of short-term mortgages – the very factors the Treasury had sought to address in the mid 2000s – proved to be the things that prevented a bigger housing market shakeout in 2008–9.

Housing market volatility may now be reduced by the greater ability of the Bank of England (via the FPC) to intervene to prevent financial instability. But it will also depend on whether the whole economy can be kept on a stable path. Even if the new regulatory institutions work smoothly together in the UK context, there will be shocks from developments in the world economy that affect UK financial markets. With house prices rising relative to incomes, the household debt/income ratio will inevitably rise unless the rate of owner-occupation falls. A high household debt to income ratio is not necessarily a problem, but the potential risks that accompany it need to be managed. And it is vital that the housing market itself is sufficiently resilient to cope with whatever shocks it encounters. This concern underpins the next chapter.

Chapter 5

Risk in the housing market

The cliché 'safe as houses' sums up the security that 'home' conjures up for most of us from childhood, and the widespread view that housing represents a safe store of wealth. But what is the balance between rationality and risk with regard to home ownership? Should the government do more to help manage households' risk?

Opinions about house purchase vary according to recent trends in house prices relative to other assets. The house price falls in the early 1990s reduced confidence in bricks and mortar. By the end of that decade the dot-com boom meant that investment in the equity market was favoured. However, in the early 2000s preferences shifted back toward the housing market as the equity market fell sharply from its peak in late 1999 through to 2002, the bank rate was cut from 6% in early 1999 to a low of 3.5% in mid 2003, and new housing supply fell to a low in 2001.

These factors sowed the seeds of the long house price upswing, which then ran almost continuously until 2007. But while housing wealth in the UK is a relatively large proportion of household financial assets, real investment in housing is rather low. Dwellings investment peaked at just 4.6% of UK output in the 2000s. In the US the peak was 6.5% and in Ireland 14%. Meanwhile, in France the peak was

6.7% and in Germany the proportion was steady between 5% and 6%.

Is it a concern if UK households put their money into housing?

Does the flow of finance into housing divert investment from more productive uses? If so, it might mean the UK had a relatively low level of business investment and/or that UK businesses faced relatively high interest rates. And indeed total investment in the UK tends to be lower relative to GDP than in France and Germany (although the share is similar to that in the US).

Many large firms in the UK will be able to borrow overseas, so it is small businesses that are most likely to be harmed if too large a share of savings goes to residential investment. It has for decades been argued that there is too little finance available for UK small and medium-sized enterprises, which have to rely on short-term bank lending.[44] There is also evidence that real short- and long-term interest rates in the UK have been relatively high since 1980, at least compared with those in the US, France and Germany.[45]

A high rate of home ownership could, in theory, be good for entrepreneurship, as people will be able to use the equity in their homes as collateral when seeking bank loans. But, in practice, those with relatively high levels of mortgage debt are less likely to start businesses.[39]

Unfortunately, while it may be undesirable for the whole economy to have so much of people's savings flow into housing, for many households this is an entirely rational decision. The uncertainties of the economic cycle make it difficult to rely on financial investments as the only provision for the needs of old age, whereas home ownership is a pretty good hedge against the cost of shelter in retirement. In addition, the emotional connotations of 'home' mean that housing assets can be regarded differently from financial assets: for example, in the means test for social care at home the value of the home is disregarded.

This rational incentive is even more problematic when households acquire housing space that exceeds their actual 'needs' (or remain in large houses when family size reduces) partly because they expect to benefit from future price increases. Apart from the question of 'fair shares' of housing space, this decision does carry risk. There is less certainty about the value of a specific house than about the housing market as a whole. Besides, not only are there ups and downs, but we cannot assume that house prices will always rise more than alternative investments in the long term. Over time population and income trends may alter locally, regionally or even nationally, and this will affect house prices.

Do people realize the risks of home ownership?

High housing debt relative to household income in the UK increases the financial vulnerability of many households. Long-term returns on the UK housing market have been similar to those on equities, and they have been less volatile.[46] But while most people will invest in a range of equities, they will typically invest in only a single house: a riskier approach to investment. Households borrow a lot to do so, and may underestimate the costs of repair and maintenance that go with home ownership.

There is good evidence that people often do not fully understand their mortgage contracts and the risks of house purchase. Better financial education would need to counter both the inevitable emotion involved in acquiring a home and behaviour during housing booms, when expectations of future price rises encourage people to rush in.

As already explained, the role of the new financial regulators, ensuring mortgages are more sustainable for households, should help. However, unexpected changes in personal circumstances mean risk remains for both borrowers and lenders. Even in the stable economy of the ten years to 2007/8, the main reason for mortgage arrears was loss of income, accounting for around 65% of cases, with a further 25–30% resulting from household changes such as divorce. Careful lending criteria will not prevent all repossessions.

There have been fewer repossessions since the financial crisis than during the previous housing market downturn in 1991, due not only to low interest rates but also to the fact that unemployment rose a little less sharply. Repossessions peaked in 2009 at around 50,000 a year (0.43% of the stock), whereas in 1991 the peak was 75,000 (0.77%). However, in 2013, the Bank of England estimated that 8% of households had worryingly high mortgage payments relative to their income, and that this would rise to 16% if interest rates rose by 2.5% while household incomes remained unchanged.[47] There is much uncertainty about just how easy it will be for households to adjust to a rising interest rate environment.

Policies to limit the impact of repossessions

A flood of repossessions is not only traumatic for the households concerned: it can damage the whole housing market, it can harm the profitability of mortgage lenders and it can have political consequences. For these reasons governments often support borrowers in difficulty during downturns. In the early

1990s many lenders had taken out Mortgage Indemnity Guarantees, but the high cost of these for insurers forced the government to provide additional support for those in arrears. Later in the 1990s there was an attempt to move mortgage holders onto private insurance by tightening the conditions for state assistance.

The period of economic stability and strong employment trends reduced the inclination to take out insurance, however, so take-up was never very high. Then the scandal about the mis-selling of Payment Protection Insurance brought all forms of payment insurance into disrepute. As a result, when the financial crisis started to affect the housing market it was evident that private insurance was not going to be enough. So in 2009 a variety of changes to the Support for Mortgage Interest programme were introduced, including shortening the waiting period before it was payable to those on Jobseeker's Allowance, and increasing the size of mortgage that could be supported in this way. Concern that repossessions will pick up when interest rates rise led to a number of suggestions for improving support for those in arrears.[48] What does effective support need to consider?

- Fairness is needed between those who fall into arrears during a recession, when there are wider financial risks, and those who fall into arrears in more stable economic periods with less concern about knock-on effects.
- The extent of mortgage support should not exceed the extent of support via housing benefit for households in the private or social rented sector.
- The system needs to avoid moral hazard, so lenders and borrowers do not see the state as a fallback (a risk that should be reduced by the tighter lending criteria laid down by the 2014 Mortgage Market Review).

- The taxpayer should not subsidize a household's acquisition of an asset.
- There should be a clear framework to ensure that in a recession the right balance is reached between lenders and the interests of those households that are no longer able to sustain home ownership.

It might seem natural to introduce a compulsory insurance scheme but this would add to costs for all borrowers, including those who didn't need it. But encouraging sound payment protection insurance, meaning some incentive for households to take out insurance, must surely form part of any solution.[48]

Risks associated with the location of housing

The UK housing market has sharp regional divergences. Compared with the peak of the housing market in the third quarter of 2007, nominal prices in the UK as a whole were down about 10% in early 2014. But whilst in central London prices were 2% above their peak, according to the Halifax House Price Index, they were 13% below peak in Yorkshire and 16% below in the West Midlands. These divergences will conceal local idiosyncratic trends. House prices in Cambridge have risen more steeply than in the villages around Peterborough. And the price of an individual house is influenced by a variety of neighbourhood factors such as the quality of the nearest school, or a new development being built opposite. An obvious implication is that if you own a property in South Shields, it may not be that helpful in protecting against the cost of shelter in old age if for family reasons (say) you want to move to St Albans.

The riskiness associated with high borrowing to buy a specific house has prompted debate about better ways to give people the benefit of investing in housing. One suggestion is to separate 'consumption' of housing from our investment in housing.[49] A limited version of this is now offered by Castle Trust, which is selling investments in house price indexes, using the funds to finance mortgage lending with some housing market risk-sharing between lender and borrower.

Others have argued that loans including some equity investment by the lender would not only spread some of the risk from the borrower but also reduce the incentive for homebuyers to want house price increases, thereby helping to stabilize the market.[50]

Earlier schemes along these lines were not successful. However, the first part of the government's Help to Buy scheme, launched in spring 2013 for those buying new properties, is just such a scheme, in which the taxpayer provides the equity finance. This has proved popular, although there is a question about whether it is sensible to increase the taxpayers' exposure to falling house prices. Equally, it might not be good for the long-term health of the market if the government benefits from house price rises. It is probably preferable for the equity finance to come from elsewhere.

Over the past decade in particular, governments have introduced many schemes to subsidize home ownership, especially for first-time buyers. Arguably, these 'intermediate housing' policies add to demand and at the margin fuel higher prices. In addition, it is not always easy for those helped to move on into the more 'normal' market. These schemes do support purchase by occupiers rather than landlords, and may therefore help to lessen wealth inequality, but they fall far short of being an adequate solution.

Summary

There are disadvantages in people being unduly biased towards putting money into bricks and mortar. While it is rational for people to invest in housing, in particular to meet the cost of shelter in old age, there are also risks, which may not be fully appreciated, in borrowing to buy a specific house. The government should set out clearly how much taxpayer support can be expected for those who fall into mortgage arrears, and it should encourage better mortgage payment insurance. More equity finance of home buying would be welcome, but private initiatives would be preferable to the current government scheme.

In introducing reforms that change the structure of the housing market, we always need to be mindful of the potential for adverse effects on existing borrowers and homeowners. This is even more important when it comes to proposals for tax reform.

Chapter 6

Taxing questions

Tax reforms are often urged as the solution to the perceived shortcomings of the housing market. But radical changes in tax must meet a very high bar to have any prospect of success. So many people have their wealth tied up in housing that changes have to be sensitive to their reasonable expectations. Any tax reform needs to command wide political support, be very thoroughly justified, and its benefits must be clearly articulated. It can be done: one example is the phasing out of Mortgage Interest Relief at Source in the 1990s, which had been regarded as politically impossible.

The recent Mirrlees Review of the UK tax system set out an economic approach to taxation, and this chapter draws on its insights.[51] It describes the key principles of good taxes:

- they should have as little impact as possible on welfare and economic efficiency;
- they should not be unduly costly to administer or comply with;
- they should be fair in procedure, discrimination between groups, and have regard to legitimate expectations; and
- they should be transparent – people should be able to understand the tax system.

I would also argue that the tax system should promote fairness in the distribution of income and wealth.

Proposals to reform housing or development taxation usually have one of the following aims in mind:

- to reduce the incentive for households to speculate on rising prices and so reduce both house price volatility and possibly the level of prices;
- to move towards a more equal distribution of wealth;
- to move towards a better distribution of housing space;
- to achieve a 'level playing field' between tenure types;
- to achieve a 'level playing field' between housing and other assets;
- to stimulate more housebuilding; and
- to support environmental goals.

This chapter looks at present and proposed taxes in the UK, starting with taxes on households and moving on to the taxation of landowners and developers. Today's system has evident weaknesses, assessed against the aims listed above. But it is hard to produce remedies that don't either have adverse unintended consequences or run up against the broad principles of good taxation. And that is before considering the politics.

What might we want to tax? We can think of owner-occupied housing as providing two conceptually separate benefits. One is the obvious flow of 'housing services' (the benefits to the occupants of having somewhere to live), and the other is the investment element (the rise and fall in the asset value, which reflects changes in the value of the land on which the dwelling stands). In principle these should be taxed differently, but in practice they are hard to distinguish.

There are also two elements that might be taxed with regard to new development. One is the gain in the land price when planning permission is granted (for the landowner), and the other is the environmental cost of developing that particular site (for the purchaser of the dwelling).

Stamp duty land tax (SDLT)

SDLT is charged on housing transactions and paid by the purchaser (in the sense that they sign the cheque; but this means they will pay less for the property, so the actual burden of taxation is shared between the seller and the buyer). It is a 'slab' tax, so that a property costing £124,999 attracts no tax, but one costing £125,001 attracts a tax of 1% on the whole price. At the time of writing the rate rises in stages, reaching 7% for properties over £2 million, with lower rates for properties in certain disadvantaged areas.

SDLT gets short shrift in the Mirrlees Review: 'transaction taxes are particularly inefficient' and 'this is, of course, an absurd structure for any tax'. Most economists agree. So is there any case for its retention?

If stamp duty were simply abolished, the revenue would need to be raised somewhere else. SDLT on residential property raised £4.9 billion in 2012/13 and this is projected to rise to £14.9 billion in 2018/19. But an alternative form of taxation would probably be more economically efficient.

However, there are some reasons to think it is a useful tax to retain. Receipts are anti-cyclical: that is, they rise in periods of strong economic growth, taking money out of the economy, and vice versa. It is a reasonably easy tax to adjust as needed. It could, for example, be tried as part of any effort to deflate a housing 'bubble', by increasing the rate of duty on higher-priced properties.

A very desirable reform would be to change the structure of SDLT so that the higher rates are charged only on the margin above each threshold. This would mean that it would no longer have a distorting effect on prices around the thresholds. But to take it out of the tax armoury altogether would be to lose a useful weapon.

Capital gains tax (CGT) and inheritance tax (IHT)

CGT is not charged on a household's main dwelling, but it is charged on second homes and on rented properties. The exemption was brought into some disrepute when the scandal about MPs' expenses revealed the scope for 'flipping' the designation of the main dwelling. Tightening up the CGT regime in this respect would seem uncontroversial.

More radically, charging CGT on gains on our main residences would bring the taxation of housing more into line with other assets, and it would tend to discourage over-investment in housing. This reform would tackle directly some of the biggest concerns arising from our present housing market.

But it would bring with it a number of complications. If it is charged on every transaction a household makes, then there is a real disincentive to move. However, if the tax is rolled up on a sequence of housing transactions over a lifetime, divorce and downsizing raise problems. Each taxpayer would need to have a record of their CGT liability, which would be payable at the time of 'last sale' in the housing market (often on death). This means that an assessment of the tax would need to be made on every move, and would have to take into account improvements: for example, the cost of an extension would need to be added to the purchase price, and distinguishing improvements from maintenance could also prove pretty complex. In addition, the charge might need to be reduced to take account of only house price rises above inflation.

Even so, the case for applying CGT to housing is strong. Changes in house prices often result from public policy: restrictions on neighbouring land, transport links, or the quality of a nearby school, for example. It is odd not to tax these gains, which the homeowner has done nothing to earn, but charge CGT on the profits from selling a business enterprise. But it would undoubtedly face very strong public, and therefore political, opposition.

Given that first homes are already exempt from CGT, a bizarre argument in relation to IHT is that the tax thresholds should be increased as house prices rise. This reflects the importance attached to the ability of a family that benefited from higher house prices to pass this on to subsequent generations, often enabling them to enter the housing market in their turn. But it is unclear whether lowering the IHT threshold would attract more or less opposition than charging CGT on the main dwelling, as IHT is itself highly unpopular. This would also be less well targeted on housing assets.

IHT and CGT could be considered as alternative approaches to taxing the windfall that accrues to existing homeowners from living in a country where development is constrained. Since there are well-known difficulties in establishing an effective tax take for IHT, especially from the very wealthy, this suggests that the best approach would be a CGT charge on housing rolled up by an individual or couple over their lifetimes to be charged on the death of the second partner, as for IHT, and for the amount charged in this way to be subtracted from the estate for IHT purposes.

This reform could lower the rate of housing inflation (as the effective tax take on owner-occupation is increased) and reduce the incentive to hold housing assets for investment motives. It would improve equality by increasing the ability of those not fortunate enough to inherit a share of a property to compete in the housing market. With digital records, complex administration should not stand in the way of this reform.

In order not to disrupt the housing market, it would be best to start from the housing values prevailing when the CGT regime was introduced. There would therefore be a slow build-up in revenue, meaning the government brave enough to introduce this new tax would take all the opprobrium while the benefits of a larger flow of tax revenues and more equal access to home ownership would only emerge over succeeding decades. Even an optimist about tax reform might feel daunted by this, and yet it may well be the best reform to tackle the adverse social consequences of undersupply of housing.

Taxation of rental property versus home ownership

As discussed earlier, the private rented sector has grown and in terms of taxation the aim should be for a 'level playing field' between this sector and owner-occupation. Whether buy-to-let landlords enjoy undue tax advantages relative to owner-occupiers is a debated point. The Mirrlees Report argued that, since both rental income and capital gains are taxed on rental properties, this tenure is in fact overtaxed relative to owner-occupation.

On the other hand, a recent report from the Intergenerational Foundation suggested that the tax allowance for 'wear and tear' and the ability of landlords to evade CGT means that landlords are actually undertaxed.[52]

As with many tax questions, it is important to think about where the burden of tax effectively falls rather than looking at who pays it in the first instance. Landlords seek to make a return, including any element of capital gains, that is equivalent to that on alternative investments. Indeed, one reason for house price rises in the low interest rate era is that modest returns on alternative investments have meant that landlords are prepared to accept a lower rental yield (rents divided by the capital cost of the dwelling). So taxing landlords more could push up rents in the short term while pushing down on the price for buy-to-let properties and thus benefiting those wanting to enter the housing market as owner-occupiers. But the higher rents would be adverse for those left in the private rented sector: often those who already have most financial stress due to the burden of their housing costs.

Rent levels obviously also depend on what tenants can afford. This was the rationale for the move by the 2010 coalition government to cap housing benefits relative to the rent level in any area, preventing landlords effectively exploiting the government's ability to pay. Rents in the unsubsidized market sector might plausibly be expected to reflect the incomes of those who either don't wish to have the responsibility or permanency of home ownership, or are not in a financial position to qualify for a mortgage. If there were a sufficient supply of dwellings, and a reasonable share of the market was private rental, then market forces would keep rents at a level that was more affordable for such households.

Major reform to the taxation of landlords does not seem desirable. But a limited reform consisting of a robust attempt to close any loopholes in CGT for buy-to-let landlords, and a stronger regulatory regime to improve standards in the private rented sector, would respond to concerns about landlords reaping undue profits.

VAT on new-build housing

The UK is unusual in applying a zero rate of VAT to the construction of residential property, but since VAT is essentially a tax on consumption, this is appropriate. Taxing the consumption of a long-lasting good at the point of purchase is not correct, and a better alternative is using the annual council tax to tax the consumption of 'housing services'.

However, there is a big anomaly in that VAT is charged on renovations and extensions, creating a tax incentive toward demolition and rebuilding, or new construction, as opposed to renovating and extending existing property. There are two possible ways to tackle this.

- Charge a reduced rate of VAT both on new build and on renovations at a level designed to keep the tax take broadly unchanged. But the objection to charging any VAT on new building remains, and this would run against EU rules on VAT.
- Charge a zero rate of VAT on renovations. This is theoretically the most satisfactory solution and would provide an incentive to extend the present stock so that areas would tend to become denser in terms of population per hectare. It would have the complication that the relief should only apply to significant building projects (simple redecoration, replacement of windows, and so on ought not to qualify). And it would imply a loss of tax revenue as well as benefiting the wealthy installing basements in London. Nevertheless, I would argue that this should form part of a package of housing tax reform as it would stimulate housing supply while using land efficiently. Distributional impacts could be offset elsewhere.

Council tax

The unhappy experience of the poll tax has left successive governments reluctant to reform council tax, even in
the face of good arguments for doing so. For example, a
set of sensible, though not far-reaching, reforms of council tax proposed by Sir Michael Lyons in his 2007 government-sponsored inquiry has generally not been taken forward.[53] This is also an unpopular tax as it is highly visible;
tax transparency may be theoretically desirable but it can
provoke resistance.

There are two kinds of problem with the present council
tax. More minor issues concern the unfairness of the system
due to a failure to undertake a revaluation of the housing
stock and to the lesser rate of taxation compared with value
for more expensive properties. Those living in local authorities where house prices have been relatively weak – often
poorer areas – tend to be overtaxed. Those in high-value
properties are undertaxed due to the width of the highest
council tax band.

There is some political willingness to contemplate reform of the upper council tax bands – the 'mansion tax'
supported at times by Labour and by the Liberal Demo-
crats is a different approach to the same issue. A recent
thorough discussion of council tax reform suggested that
a move to a council tax more closely linked to property values would have some redistributive impacts, though at the
cost of a major disadvantage for low-income households
in London.[54] However, there is little political appetite for
frequent revaluations.

Reform of the upper bands would still leave the major
problem of the tensions between the various roles that council tax plays. Council tax is to some extent all of the following:

- a substitute for VAT on the consumption of housing services;
- a proxy for a land value tax on the area a dwelling occupies;
- a source of independent and accountable finance for local government; and
- a charge for local services.

One tax cannot do all of these things well.

- To be a good proxy for VAT, council tax would have to move in line with imputed rents. Further improvements in the collection of rental data to enable production of the new CPIH (consumer price index including owner-occupied housing costs) might enable local authorities to adjust council tax in line with rental movements. This certainly does not happen now.
- To be a good proxy for a land value tax, council tax would have to vary with land prices. But land prices are very variable (they rose sharply in the run-up to the financial crisis, and then fell back). This volatility would make this a poor way to finance local government.
- While in its present form it is a stable source of funding, it does not increase with economic growth.
- Council tax is a very visible link between voters and their councillors but it covers only a modest proportion of the cost of local services, so small changes in local authority spending can have a big impact on council tax bills.

A very radical reform in local taxation could include the following measures.

- A shift to a local income tax to substitute for part of the present council tax, perhaps linked with a higher proportion of local services being effectively funded from local sources. The amount of tax collected would respond to economic growth and would give local authorities a better incentive to encourage economic activity.
- A local tax based on the value of only the building part of property, raising a rather smaller sum than the present council tax.
- A national property tax, varying with land values, with annual revaluations.

The benefits of this package of reforms would include reduced enthusiasm for rising land prices, and possibly less local opposition to new housing development. It would also divide up appropriately the taxation of the housing services and investment elements for homeowners. But there would be the following very significant drawbacks.

- Income tax collection would be more complex. A local income tax collected nationally and then redistributed could diminish the perceived link between the tax and the local authority.
- Land values would need to be established, and updating would not be easy. As pointed out earlier, changes in very local factors – such as a development that blocks a view – can affect relative prices of small areas.
- Public opinion polling suggests that taxes on wealth, particularly housing wealth, are seen as unfair in comparison to taxes on income. This can be countered to some extent by suggesting that taxes based on property values could be rolled up against the value of the house when sold.

Such major reform would also have an effect on relative house prices. It might have to be undertaken gradually to avoid market disruption, losses by lenders and the spread of negative equity. Overall, this would be a complex change that would achieve a theoretically better system, but with uncertain practical benefits.

More modest – but still useful – changes, such as the introduction of higher council tax bands, seem preferable. In addition, consideration could be given to removing the 25% discount for single adult occupancy in order to discourage under-occupation, although this should be combined with a greater provision of suitable new dwellings for the elderly and better support for them through the process of moving. Pushing up council tax further on long-term empty homes should also be implemented, as some councils are already doing.

Land value tax (LVT) and 'betterment' taxation

'The economic case for taxing land itself is very strong and there is a long history of arguments in favour of it. Taxing land ownership is equivalent to taxing an economic rent; to do so does not discourage any desirable activity.'

Quote taken from the Mirrlees Review[51]

In terms of fairness, an LVT on residential property, land used for commercial or agricultural purposes or, indeed, land left vacant is justified as a form of property tax. But it is a special form, as the value in land, unlike that in business property, is often not created by the individual owner.

The basic argument here was famously made by Winston Churchill in 1909:

Roads are made...electric light turns night into day...and all the while the landlord sits still... To not one of those improvements does the land monopolist...contribute, and yet by every one of them the value of his land is enhanced.

So one justification for an LVT is that landowners benefit from improvements to which they have not contributed. A particular example of this is the change in land value, usually an uplift, that results from the granting of planning permission. (Note that this might not argue strongly for a tax on agricultural land, where the farmer's work does affect land value.) The second justification is that an LVT would encourage landowners to put their land to its best use: by discouraging undeveloped urban land being left vacant in the hope of an improvement in the property market, for example.

The most straightforward form of LVT would simply tax land annually according to the value in its present use, satisfying those who believe landownership is undertaxed. Such a tax would, on introduction, automatically reduce the capital value of all land – by an amount dependent on the rate of tax – and would be very controversial if agricultural land were included. However, unless the rate of taxation was very high it might only have a marginal impact on the incentive to bring land forward for development.

Other proposed forms of LVT are aimed more directly at encouraging development. LVT could be charged on the assessed value of the land – this might include 'hope value' if a site were thought likely to gain planning permission in due course. Apart from the difficulty of agreeing the value of each site (and deciding how frequently valuations would be undertaken), there is the further problem that the hope value at any time will depend on decisions about the local plan, which are uncertain matters of public policy.

A different approach would be to tax land according to its best use given the present planning designation. This could be highly effective in urban areas – a plot being used as a car park, for example, might not be bringing in sufficient revenue to outweigh a 1% charge on its potential high value as development land. It would have a sharper impact in rural areas: if a field were brought into the development envelope but the farmer had no wish to develop it, the decision could effectively be forced upon them through financial pressures (even at a 1% rate, if a hectare of prime development land were worth £2.9 million,[55] the annual charge would be a cool £29,000).

This version of LVT would certainly discourage landowners and developers from holding potential development sites back from the market (in the hope of better times, or in order to avoid too many dwellings being built in an area at the same time). But the interaction of this tax with the planning system could also have some perverse outcomes. The local authority will have a five-year-plus supply of sites that can readily be developed for housing, but it will not want all the housing built at the same time. This would mean that some landowners would pay LVT on a high land value while having to wait before that land can be developed. There would also be a lot of pressure on local plans to be consistent about which sites were preferred for development. A decision to delay a site's permission, or a failure to deliver planned infrastructure so a site has to be mothballed, could provoke the accusation that LVT had been paid on too high a value.

Concerns about the practicalities of LVT are often met with the response that it is managed successfully elsewhere. The two examples generally cited are the US and Denmark.

In the US, an LVT has most frequently been used at a municipal level, rather than more widely. It is therefore best thought of as a tax on vacant or underutilized urban land, and it has had success in increasing densities. Used for this purpose, several of the objections identified above would be less relevant, and an LVT would be based on a stronger environmental case than if it were introduced to order to hasten greenfield land into development.

In Denmark, the public dislike for property tax caused it to be frozen in nominal terms after 2002. When it was in operation, Denmark had a more stable market than the UK in terms of house prices.

These examples illustrate that LVT is technically feasible, but they do not suggest that huge benefits flow from its introduction. LVT might be part of a move to a wider tax on all wealth, but I am unconvinced we can look to it to solve housing problems.

Taxation of sites with planning permission

Planning permissions need to be renewed after three years, with attendant costs and uncertainty, so there is already a considerable incentive for developers to build. Other incentives are the holding cost of the land itself and the administrative cost of getting the planning permission in the first place. An Office of Fair Trading report in 2008 on this topic came to the following conclusion.

> We found no evidence that individual homebuilders have persistent or widespread market power or that they are able to restrict supply or inflate prices. Having a stock of land helps a homebuilder cope with fluctuations in the housing market and also helps to reduce its exposure

to risk resulting from the planning system. We have not found any evidence that homebuilders have the ability to anti-competitively hoard land or own a large amount of land, with planning permission, on which they have not started to build. Apart from the homebuilding firms, the available information suggests that the largest 'landbank' may be that held by the public sector.[57]

Land-banking of permissioned sites is at most a minor issue. To seek to address it by taxation would raise the cost of development, and increase risk for developers. Developers would then try to time the acquisition of planning permission very close to start dates, making their businesses harder to manage. So in the event of a strong market pickup there would be more delay before construction responded, as there would be fewer outstanding permissions. This will not result in greater housing supply.

Myth 7 **There is nothing wrong with the planning system: we just need to see sites with planning permission developed**

A proposal that resurfaces regularly in the housing supply debate is a tax on unbuilt (or unstarted) housing units with planning permissions. In support of this, the 381,000 unimplemented planning permissions identified in England by the Local Government Association in 2013 are often cited.[56] However, a closer look shows that only 184,000 of these were units that had not been started. It is also often the case that a site has not been started due to the need for associated conditions (around highways, for example) to be agreed.

Summary

The taxation of land and property is a complex topic. Proposals to increase taxation need to be seen against the background that the UK already has a relatively high tax take on property at over 4% of GDP (the OECD average is under 2%), much of which is from recurrent taxes (council tax and business rates). Taking all the arguments above into account, I would propose the following package as a coherent set of tax reforms.

- Stamp duty reformed to end its 'slab' structure, and the lost revenue partly replaced with a site value tax on vacant land that is both urban and brownfield.
- Higher bands should be added to council tax, and the single adult discount should be abolished.
- VAT should be removed from major household renovations and extensions.
- There should be a check on loopholes used by buy-to-let landlords to reduce CGT payments.
- A move to charge CGT on the main residence should be made, with the charge rolled up over a lifetime.

Even without the change to CGT, this would improve the efficiency of use of urban land and of the housing stock, make council tax fairer, and stimulate transactions and housing stock improvement. The CGT change is rather more radical. Politically this seems unacceptable – yet without it the housing market is much less likely to deliver fair outcomes.

Chapter 7

Taxes and charges on development gains

Land for residential development commands a high price. According to the Valuation Office Agency, agricultural land around Cambridge was worth around £18,500 a hectare in 2010, compared with residential land at £2.9 million. Around Belfast, despite the post-2007 collapse of the housing market there, agricultural land was assessed to have an average value of just under £24,000 per hectare, compared with residential at £1.25 million.[58] Moving land from agricultural use to residential use confers a very significant gain. House prices drive land prices, not vice versa.

While these price differentials have not always been so great, since 1947 there have been frequent attempts to tax this gain, for the following reasons.

- The rise in value occurs as a result of a public sector planning decision: it is a windfall that the landowner has done little to earn.
- New dwellings inevitably create demand for extra infrastructure, which should where possible be funded from development gain.

Development taxes and charges: a short history

As discussed in chapter 1, attempts to tax the gains that result from the granting of permission for change of use have generally failed. The expectation of policy reversal often meant that these taxes simply encouraged the hoarding of land, and the high rates of tax and the complexity of assessment (given the varied characteristics of different sites) fostered avoidance efforts.

The failure of development taxes has led to the greater use of planning 'agreements'. These have been permitted since 1932 and broadly concern developer-funded facilities related to a particular development.[59] In 1991 the Planning and Compensation Act turned the agreements into obligations and also introduced the ability for the local authority to require the provision of social housing. (The term 'Section 106 (S106) agreements' arose from the relevant part of the 1991 act.) Various reforms to S106 have subsequently been made, generally preserving the principle that these charges relate in some way to the costs of the development.

Obligations are, in principle, neither an attempt to tax development gain nor a tax on the buying and selling of planning permissions (which is anathema in a plan-led system). One very successful example is the Milton Keynes 'roof tax' (basically a flat rate for dwellings of a certain size): this worked because it was announced early and covered a large area of similar sites.

By the early 2000s negotiations over S106 agreements had become a major reason for the delay in delivering development, and developers complained that the bill for S106 was often not fully known during the process of gaining planning permission. PPG3 had also included a requirement for 'affordable housing' (social rent and intermediate tenures) for developments of more than twenty-five dwellings (fifteen dwellings in London). Yet at the same time the government view was that not enough revenue was being raised by S106. In response to these issues my housing-supply review proposed a Planning Gain Supplement: effectively a tax on the uplift of land value due to the granting of planning permission, but charged at a lower rate than previous attempts at development taxation. If introduced, it would have gone alongside a restriction in the coverage of S106 agreements intended to produce more certainty.

This proposal was strongly opposed by developers. Its eventual withdrawal was partly because of this opposition and partly because, while taxing windfalls seems simple to economists, their value and timing is hard to establish in practice. In addition, the proposal became vulnerable to the risk that a lack of cross-party support would have meant that landowners would simply have held back. It was abandoned and replaced by the Community Infrastructure Levy (CIL), which aims both to raise additional revenue and to provide developers with more certainty about planning obligations.

Development taxes and charges: the present state of play

Profits on land are subject to CGT, but a combination of rollover relief and frequent (in the agricultural sector) losses that can be set against CGT mean that less tax is paid than might be expected. The main revenue raised from new development therefore comes from a combination of S106 agreements and (as it comes into effect) the CIL.

S106 agreements became an increasing source of revenue for Local Planning Authorities (LPAs) during the house price boom of the mid 2000s. In 2007/8, estimates suggest that £4.9 billion of S016 payments were agreed, £2.6 billion of which was for affordable housing. While the amount delivered in that year was less, it did include £1.3 billion for affordable housing.[60]

Following the financial crisis and the related fall in house prices, developers argued that the previously agreed S106 agreements were in some cases too onerous and had left developments unviable (meaning that there was insufficient profit for the site to be developed, or indeed that development might result in a loss). The initial response of most LPAs was to allow variance in the timing of the payments agreed but to make no changes to the amounts or to the demands for affordable housing. At the same time, the government intervened to restart sites that had been stalled post-crisis, through schemes such as Get Britain Building, which has supported finance on a number of stalled sites. In spring 2013 a new procedure was introduced whereby developers could appeal to have the affordable housing component of an existing S106 agreement reduced – this procedure sits alongside the existing ability to seek voluntary renegotiation of S106s. In 2014 consideration is being given to reintroducing a threshold, of ten units on a site, below which there will be no requirement to provide affordable housing.

LPAs are now also able to introduce a CIL, although they have no obligation to do so. This is supposed to be set at a rate that fills any gap between the infrastructure needed in an area to carry out the development in the plan and the finance that will be available from other (usually central government) sources. They should not be set so high that development is rendered 'unviable'.

When the CIL was first proposed, it was welcomed both by developers (who feared that the Planning Gain Supplement would have proved more costly) and by LPAs (who expected it to raise considerable sums). Unsurprisingly, as more details have emerged about how it is to be brought into effect it has become less popular. Developers have raised concerns about the impact on viability of some of the early CIL proposals, while LPAs find that preparing evidence for a CIL is burdensome against a background of falling house prices, which mean that revenue potential is lower.

Land prices

Discussions about the CIL have refocused attention on land prices. The recent Harman Review[61] of viability for local plans refers to ensuring that development provides a competitive return for the developer (which can reasonably be assessed). Determining appropriate land value is more problematic. There is mention of a 'land value sufficient to persuade the landowner to sell the land for the development proposed'. Later, the report recommends the 'residual land value approach', which is fleshed out as follows:

> We recommend that the Threshold Land Value is based on a premium over current use values and credible alternative use values.

There is also reference to 'the going rate', which suggests that account should be taken of recent transactions – although finding details of relevant comparators is not easy.

Similarly, the NPPF refers to a 'competitive return' to a willing landowner. Given the very large difference between agricultural and residential land prices, the unprejudiced observer might well wonder, having allowed for CGT and the costs of promoting the land into the planning system, just how a 'competitive return' might be defined. The public purse has an interest in reducing this residual land price, to extract more of the uplift in value for social purposes.

But there are serious impediments to achieving this. The first is that landowners are not generally forced to sell in a hurry. Landowners' expectations, and therefore what they are prepared to sell for, will often be based around their awareness of prices realized in similar transactions. They will not want to sell if it seems to be an unfavourable time to do so. Furthermore, any policy change designed to lower land-owner returns would only have the desired effect if it had strong cross-party support.

The second impediment is the behaviour of the public (or quasi-public) sector. Sellers of land can be characterized too readily as wealthy (or potentially wealthy) individuals, whereas in fact many land sales are made by firms, schools or universities disposing of surplus land and using the proceeds for investment in their business, or for new buildings. Some of these negotiations could be viewed as conflict over where in the public sector the revenue from residential development should be allocated. The public sector owns a good deal of land, and indeed the coalition government set itself the goal of 'releasing public sector land with capacity to deliver up to 100,000 homes between 2011 and 2015'. While a list of potential sites was also made available, it is difficult to find good information on how many of these sites have been sold, or how many dwellings have been built on them to date.

The Homes and Communities Agency is the government body charged with managing the disposal of these sites, and its documentation makes it clear that it is looking to achieve market values for the land. However, this is tempered by a commitment to carry out disposals 'on terms that promote development, economic activity and growth'.[62]

The tension between meeting the expectations of both the private sector and the public sector for value from land sales and the desire to achieve a return in terms of good infrastructure for the community affected is likely to continue. One proposal that could partly address this would be to look at the possibility of developing new settlements, acquiring the land for the public sector from willing sellers (as there would be less prospect of gain through the normal planning system) or, where necessary, using a Compulsory Purchase Order, in the same way as is done for major infrastructure projects. This process could be carried out by a publicly established stand-alone entity that would raise funding and then manage the development of the site in such a way as to repay the debt and establish high-quality public spaces. The public sector would own the sites and could choose to establish equity-share relationships with developers as homes are constructed. This is linked to the Garden City concept: the government published a prospectus for these in spring 2014, although it is not yet clear how successful this will prove.

New settlements, however, are not uncontentious. Some landowners may be reluctant to sell even if the financial deal is advantageous. And however well-designed the new community, and however carefully chosen the site, there will be congestion issues, and environmental and landscape questions will need to be tackled – no site will avoid some adverse impact.

Local authorities and the land market

In countries where there has been a more adequate rate of new build in response to demand, the public sector often plays a bigger role in 'land assembly' (putting together plots of land into development sites). In addition, they are often more able to borrow to fund projects. Enabling local authorities to play a bigger role might help to push supply up, although so far not many local authorities have used the extent of the financial headroom they already have, partly due to inexperience in development.

Summary

Over recent decades, various attempts have been made to ensure that the gains from the granting of planning permission by the public sector are not appropriated privately to an excessive extent. These attempts are bedevilled by two problems: complexity because each site is different, meaning that simple taxes or levies do not work well; and the ability of many landowners to hold back if they expect better times ahead, from either a taxation perspective or for wider economic reasons. The new CIL has proved difficult to introduce but has the merit of getting LPAs to produce costed infrastructure plans. (It might provoke a better debate about what infrastructure needs to be funded by central government, and also about how more infrastructure decisions could be taken locally.) Both the CIL and S106 agreements, if imposed at too high a level, raise the risk of lower quality developments, including when it comes to design.

But the fundamental issue remains, which is how to change the expectations and incentives for landowners so that more land is available for housing, and residential planning permission does not bring such sky-high gains. Part of the answer could lie in the tax changes proposed earlier, lessening the expectation that house prices will always rise in the long term. Part might also lie in the development of new, stand-alone settlements to compete with the urban fringe settlements where much development takes place at present.

Chapter 8

What would good look like?

A decade ago, when I led the the review of housing supply
for government, I was dispirited by the wide range of
problems in the housing market. Since then, the financial crisis has resulted in a severe downturn in supply and a worrying
loss of capacity in the homebuilding industry, but there have
been considerable improvements in planning policy, culminat-
ing in the introduction of the NPPF. And the regulation of the
mortgage market has been strengthened. But new residential
development is still often unwelcome, and the housing market remains a source of inequality: in dwelling space and in
location. Here I propose a package of policies to improve the
workings of the housing market. We cannot make it perfect,
but we can surely make it better.

Back to the start: what do we want from the housing market? This is my (long) wish-list.

- Households should be able to afford a decent home,
  with adequate space.
- Households should be able to move readily – to bigger
  or smaller homes, or to a different region.
- There should be a better spatial balance of economic
  activity across the UK, to avoid the costs of economic
  deprivation and urban decay (this has to be traded off

against the cost of some productivity loss as it implies less agglomeration of economic activity).

- There needs to be a well-regulated private rented sector.
- There needs to be access to social housing for those in need.
- Access to home ownership should be more equitable between those who inherit housing assets and those who do not.
- There need to be well-designed houses in areas that promote community/social life, have good public infrastructure and access to green space.
- The density of build should balance considerations of liveability against sustainable transport.
- We need a planning system that responds to market signals.
- Development location should preserve important landscapes and biodiversity.
- We need a less volatile housing market with sound mortgage lending.
- The costs and benefits of new development should be more equitably distributed.
- The benefits of infrastructure investment also need to be more equitably distributed.

This is not a controversial list, though there are elements that some people would dispute, especially with regard to density and spatial balance. The list deliberately omits any mention of a desirable rate of owner-occupation. But to respond adequately, policymakers need to recognize and make explicit some key realities and trade-offs in the housing market. We cannot achieve all of the above, so where should we compromise? How far should striking the balance be left to local decisions rather than national ones?

Four key points

The following factors, taken together, are why the UK's housing problems are intractable.

Demand for housing space rises strongly with income in the UK: as we get richer, we want more and bigger dwellings. If for environmental or 'Nimby' reasons it is not possible to build enough new dwellings – as is the case particularly in the southern part of the UK – the price of space will rise. Between 2009 and 2014 the Halifax has estimated that the average house price per square metre rose by 13% across the UK, about the same as the more usual house price index. The effects of this will be the following social ills, which we should seek to minimize.

- The better-off will continue to be able to afford the space they would like.
- The poorer will need larger subsidies per household if they are to continue to be housed decently (and more households may need subsidy), so the cost to the taxpayer will increase.
- Those just above the subsidy level will find they have to share more and have smaller dwellings than they would like.
- An increasing gap will emerge between those who inherit housing wealth and those who do not (the latter includes those whose parents have used housing wealth for their own care in old age).
- There will still be a significant incentive for households to regard housing as an investment.

Nimbyism is often a rational response to nearby development proposals. These may change the character of a place, put pressure on infrastructure, block views and occupy valued greenfield or brownfield space. It is sometimes argued that better design or (in rural areas) limiting dwellings to residents with local connections will reduce opposition. But these factors will not end it. More radical approaches might imply more direct financial benefits for households, generally through lower council tax. This could be powerful, although so far the evidence is that the New Homes Bonus (payments to councils) has not had a major effect in lessening opposition to development.

The availability of land remains the fundamental problem. We need to have sufficient land released with planning permission, and also reduce landowners' expectations about how much of the benefit of increased values they will get. But we need to be clear: landowners being prepared to accept lower prices will reduce house prices only if this is linked with an expansion of supply. Otherwise it would increase the amount available for the public sector via S106 agreements, CIL and affordable homes (though that is not a bad outcome either).

There is no easy or costless solution to the regional imbalances in the UK. London's status as a major international city, with political power, a vibrant cultural life and high-level economic activity, is inevitably going to keep much development pressure on the South East. Long-running attempts to halt economic decline in the more northern cities have had mixed results.[63] It is unlikely that every town and city can become successful.

The opposition to new development in the South East, set against the pace of potential population growth and rising incomes, makes it questionable that the rate of new dwelling supply will keep up with unconstrained demand in this and other parts of southern England. That may be the right outcome, for environmental and social reasons, although no coherent evidence for this has yet been produced. Nevertheless, it is vital that the present very low rate of new supply in England moves back towards or above 200,000 a year to ameliorate the social ills spelt out above. The policy recommendations below are aimed at a combination of a boost to housing supply, greater fairness and limiting the investment motive for owning housing. But they do not try to address the intractable problem of moving economic activity to spread it more widely across the country.

Policy recommendations

Local housing plans

A radical approach to boosting housing supply would be to localize the costs and benefits of housing subsidies and labour immobility, as proposed in a recent report by the Institute for Public Policy Research.[64] However, this involves increased national/local finance complexity. A simpler alternative is to pursue the present arrangement of giving strong encouragement to local authorities to produce sound housing plans, to ensure that the planning activity in local authorities is well funded, and to use the local government finance system to reward effective planning for appropriate growth. Local authorities could also be given greater borrowing powers (although the risk would have to lie with the authority and not the government), encouraging them to play a bigger role in land assembly. The alternative of taking more planning responsibility away from local authorities seems to me fundamentally anti-democratic. Better to set the arguments about housing supply clearly in front of communities.

There is no need for further radical planning change following the introduction of the NPPF, which will take time to have full effect. Indeed such change would be undesirable. But stronger central oversight of local authority cooperation on housing supply is needed. And green belt boundary reviews will need to play a role.

Planners and economic signals

Producing plans is a curious activity. A plan looks ahead over a period that is sufficiently long that many of the underlying assumptions are bound to prove inaccurate. Clearly, therefore, plans need to have flexibility. Rather than judging the success of a plan on whether or not it is delivered (which would be very self-referential), it should be judged in terms of outcomes such as housing waiting lists, adequate special needs housing and, crucially, house price and rental affordability. These are challenging but necessary issues for planners to tackle alongside their other key role of preserving the quality of a place. The costs of not meeting demand, in terms of higher house prices and/or limiting a city's economic potential, need to be factored into decisions.

Direct financial incentives

If Nimbyism is rational for households, can some plausible counterweight be found? The New Homes Bonus introduced by the coalition government in 2010 is a welcome step, but it has so far had only a modest impact on the willingness of local councils to become pro-development, and an even smaller impact on their voters. Policies that could shift attitudes include direct payments to those affected by the development process (dust, noise, traffic), and the ability to apply for council tax reduction readily if a view is adversely affected to a significant extent.

New settlements and urban extensions

New settlements of a substantial size, probably in the South East or the Midlands, command support across the political spectrum, and locating them away from existing settlements could reduce the level of opposition. If the public sector is able to act strongly in the land market and set up off-balance-sheet funding for early infrastructure, these would be very practical propositions.[65] However, the experience of the eco-towns proposal in the late 2000s suggests that finding acceptable sites for such projects is not easy; and the infrastructure bills will be high. The Garden City prospectus will require some political energy if it is to result in progress. It might also need new sources of finance, including from local authority or development corporation borrowing to finance the infrastructure. And it is worth noting that the build rate for Milton Keynes was just 2,500 dwellings a year. We would need a lot of new settlements to make much impact on the supply shortfall. Urban extensions will be needed too.

Self-build

Encouragement for self-build should be included as public sector land is developed. There might be a little less resistance to self-build than to developments by major house-builders – but it will only add to supply if the overall rate of land release rises, obviously. It may, however, entail sites being used less 'efficiently' in land terms as high dwelling densities may be harder to achieve.

The mortgage market

Volatility in the housing market brings risks for developers as well as for households. It raises the cost of development finance and leads to recurrent issues with the supply chain in terms of skills, the supply of materials and industry capacity (a large number of small and medium-sized residential builders disappeared during the financial crisis). The tighter regulation of mortgages by the Financial Conduct Authority (FCA) and the greater scrutiny of systemic risks in lending ought to reduce this volatility. But it should be noted that the aims of these reforms are the protection of borrowers and financial stability, not the reduction of house price volatility. The retention of stamp duty as a further countercyclical housing market tool may be wise.

Taxing undeveloped land

As proposed in chapter 5 as one of the suggested tax reforms, undeveloped urban brownfield land should be taxed in order to encourage it to be brought forward for residential (or business) use.

VAT and council tax reform

Both the removal of VAT from major renovations and an increase in council tax bands for high-value homes should have a modest impact on the use of the existing housing stock. If young people return home for several years after university, or if elder care is best done in a shared house, the ability to extend to make this kind of family living acceptable becomes important. As it becomes more expensive to finance single-person households, it is increasingly questionable to assume that we should add small dwellings to the existing stock.

Capital gains tax on main residence

If objections to development lead to some effective rationing, then it seems perverse not to tax the benefit to owner-occupiers that comes from price increases for the existing stock. If politicians are not prepared to face up to the need for much more housebuilding, they must instead face up to taxing capital gains on housing.

Risk-sharing in mortgage finance

The present system of mortgage finance is risky for the mortgagee, the mortgagor and the taxpayer (given that in times of crisis the government will often need to step in to support those in danger of losing their homes). Shared equity finance (with risk in individual houses more widely spread) and a return to a better-regulated mortgage insurance system offer ways to disperse this risk – risk that could otherwise be exacerbated by speculative behaviour based on the assumption of ever-rising prices. In addition, government needs to be clear and consistent about how much support can be expected for those who fall into arrears.

Regulation of the rental market

The rental market will continue to play a significant role, and the taxpayer will continue to subsidize a greater share of private rents as the housing benefit bill increases along with the price of housing space. Against this background, stronger regulation of quality and financial fairness in the sector will become more important. Wholesale rent control is not an attractive option, but making it easier to challenge unduly high rents and encouraging longer rental periods, with control of rent increases, would make the sector more suitable for families.

A holistic approach

Rather than being a story of steady progress, the history of housing policy is one of often knee-jerk responses to the economic cycle or to public spending pressures, meaning that a variety of policies are deployed in turn. A more coherent approach would require a steadier view of long-term or medium-term goals for managing the issues of spatial development and housing supply, with planning policy and regulatory regimes firmly directed towards those goals. A different set of tools should be kept in store for tackling the inevitable cyclical pressures: these would include the management of lending (by the FPC and the PRA), the management of forbearance (by the PRA and the FCA), possible changes to stamp duty (by HM Treasury) and mortgage rescue schemes (by HM Treasury, the Department for Communities and Local Government and the Department for Work and Pensions).

The sentence above demonstrates just how many regulators, committees and departments have their fingers in the housing policy pie. When the long-term goals of housing policy are considered, the Department of Health could be added to the list, along with all local authorities, looking at the needs of the disabled and elderly and the ill-effects on health at all ages of indecent housing or badly designed communities.

From time to time there have been ministerial committees with a housing policy focus. Such a group, which would now include the governor of the Bank of England and the chief executive of the FCA, ought to have permanent existence and some supporting structure. Since many of the risks and opportunities in housing ultimately have large implications for public finance, the Chancellor of the Exchequer would be a natural chair for such a committee. In addition, the ministerial committee should be offered independent public advice by a group of experts (a more rounded version of the ill-fated National Housing and Planning Advice Unit) in order to ensure that the tensions betwen the overall goals and the desires of the various government departments are played out explicitly. The costs of housing undersupply would then be brought into stark focus.

Endnotes

1. Martin Wolf, *Financial Times*, 13 October 2013.

2. Department of Communities and Local Government. 2007. Homes for the future: more affordable, more sustainable. Command 7191 (July).

3. A household is defined as one or more people who share a dwelling unit (flat or house). Cheaper housing means more households form for the same total population, as there is less sharing.

4. A. Shlay. 2012. Life, liberty and the pursuit of housing. Conference Paper presented at After the Crisis: Housing Policy and Finance in the US and UK, New School, New York (September).

5. A good account of the issues here is set out in A. Oswald. 1999. The housing market and Europe's unemployment: a non-technical paper. University of Warwick (May).

6. Sir Adrian Montague. 2012. Review of the barriers to institutional investment in private rented homes. Department of Communities and Local Government (August).

7. This question is reviewed in the papers on the Consumer Prices Advisory Committee section of the Office of National Statistics website. (Consumer Prices Advisory Committee. 2012. Decision on the recommended approach to incorporating owner occupiers' housing costs in an expanded consumer prices index (14 April).)

8. A. Bertaud. 2014. Cities as labour markets. Working Paper 2, Marron Institute, New York.

9. Just how hard it is to work against prevailing spatial economic pressures is set out in P. Cheshire, M. Nathan and H. Overman. 2014. *Urban Economics and Urban Policy*. Edward Elgar.

10. A good discussion of spatial policy for England as a whole can be found in Hetherington Commission. 2006. Connecting England. Town and Country Planning Association.

11. The account of planning history here draws heavily on B. Cullingworth and V. Nadin. 2006. *Town and Country Planning in the UK*, 14th edn. Routledge.

12. A great account of the background debates here, from which it is clear that there is nothing new about opposition to development, can be found in D. Kynaston. 2007. *Austerity Britain 1945–51*. Bloomsbury.

13. These data are drawn from the 'live tables' on the Department of Communities and Local Government website. It should be noted that the definitional and other changes mean that the data for earlier decades may not be exact comparators.

14. Savills Research. 2014. Planning countdown to the next election.

15. M. Stephens, C. Whitehead and M. Munro. 2005. Lessons from the past, challenges for the future for housing policy. Office of the Deputy Prime Minister (January).

16. An externality here is a cost that is imposed on others (e.g. pollution) that the person or firm creating the cost does not pay for.

17. Friends of the Earth. 2011. Draft national planning policy framework: failing to plan for the future?

18. Cullingworth and Nadin (2006).

19. A narrative on planning theory is Y. Rydin. 2003. *Urban and Environmental Planning in the UK*. Palgrave Macmillan.

20. Founder of Mass Observation, quoted in Kynaston (2007).

21. The 2001-based projection underneath the table is for England as a whole as the Department of Communities and Local Government no longer publishes data on a regional basis.

22. A. Holmans, with C. Whitehead. 2008. New and higher projections of the population. Tomorrow Series Paper 10, Town and Country Planning.

23. The 2007 guidance for Strategic Housing Market Assessments underlies the recently updated and much-improved Planning Policy Guidance.

24. See the discussion in Cheshire et al. (2014).

25. T. Auterson. 2014. Forecasting house prices. Working Paper 6, Office for Budget Responsibility (July).

26. P. Cheshire. 2014. Turning houses into gold: the failure of British planning. Centre Piece, Centre for Economic Performance, LSE (Spring).

27. K. Barker. 2006. Barker review of land use planning. Interim Report – Analysis, HM Treasury (December).

28. Office of the Deputy Prime Minister. 2005. A sustainability impact study of additional housing scenarios in England (December).

29. K. Barker. 2004. Delivering stability: securing our future housing needs. Final report: recommendations. HM Treasury (March).

30. Office of the Deputy Prime Minister. 2005. Government response to Kate Barker's review of housing supply: the supporting analysis (December).

31. Foresight. 2010. Land use futures: making the most of land in the 21st century. Government Office for Science.

32. A step forward here is UK National Ecosystem Assessment. 2011. Synthesis of key findings. UNEA–WCMC, Cambridge.

33. Although Cheshire et al. (2014) has a good, and sceptical, account of the efforts to regenerate failing places.

34. A good discussion of these issues can be found in G. Bramley. 2013. Housing market models and planning. In *Town Planning Review*, volume 84(1).

35. Cambridge Centre for Housing and Planning Research. 2014. The nature of planning constraints. Report to the Department for Communities and Local Government Committee (March).

36. A. Penfold. 2010. Review of non-planning consents. Report, Department for Business, Innovation & Skills (July).

37. D. Miles. 2004. The UK mortgage market: taking a longer-term view. HM Treasury (March).

38. For example, a recent study has suggested a price elasticity of supply of just 0.5 in the UK, compared with 2.1 in Germany, 1.1 in France and 1.4 in the US. See J. Swank, J. Kakes and A. F. Tieman. 2002. The housing ladder, taxation and borrowing constraints. De Nederlandsche Bank. A. Caldera and A. Johansson. 2013. The price responsiveness of housing supply in OECD countries. *Journal of Housing Economics*, volume 22.

39. P. Bracke, C. Hilber and O. Silva. 2013. Homeownership and entrepreneurship: the role of commitment and mortgage debt. Discussion Paper 7417, Institute for the Study of Labour, Bonn (May).

40. A good summary of the main arguments here is W. Buiter. 2009. Housing wealth isn't wealth. Discussion Paper 2009-56, Economics E-journal.

41. This is set out in more detail in M. Stephens. 2011. Tackling housing market volatility in the UK. Joseph Rowntree Foundation (May).

42. These questions are discussed in K. Barker. 2012. Macroeconomic policy: too much autonomy and too little coordination. Centre Forum (August). Sir Andrew Large. 2013. Letter to Andrew Tyrie, Treasury Committee Chairman (December).

43. A good summary of the changes at the Bank of England is given by E. Murphy and S. Senior. 2013. Changes to the Bank of England. Bank of England Quarterly Bulletin (Q1).

44. This issue is outlined in A. Posen. 2009. Getting credit flowing: a non-monetarist approach to quantitative easing. Speech at Cass Business School (October).

45. K. Barker. 2009. Stability, instability and monetary policy. Speech to South London Business (March).

46. Pension Commission. 2004. Pensions: challenges and choices, the first report. Appendices (p. 68). The Stationery Office.

47. P. Bunn and M. Rostom. 2013. The financial position of British households: evidence from the 2013 NMG Consulting Survey. Bank of England Quarterly Bulletin, volume 53(4).

48. A good summary of this is given in S. Wilcox and P. Williams. 2013. Building an effective safety net for homeowners and the housing market: unfinished business. Joseph Rowntree Foundation (July).

49. S. J. Smith. 2010. Care-full markets: miracle or mirage. Tanner Lectures, Clare Hall, Cambridge (November).

50. D. Miles. 2013. Housing, leverage and the wider economy. Speech at the Federal Reserve Bank of Dallas (November).

51. Institute for Fiscal Studies. 2011. Tax by Design – Mirrlees Review (November).

52. D. Kingman. 2013. Why BTL equals 'big tax let-off'. Intergenerational Foundation (November).

53. Sir Michael Lyons. 2007. Lyons inquiry into local government. The Stationery Office (March).

54. C. Leishman et al. 2014. After the council tax: impacts of property tax reform on people, places and house prices. Joseph Rowntree Foundation (March).

55. Price of residential land in Cambridge in 2010, according to the Valuation Office Agency.

56. Local Government Association. 2013. An analysis of unimplemented planning permissions for residential dwellings (October).

57. Office of Fair Trading. 2008. Homebuilding in the UK: a market study. OFT 1020 (September).

58. The VOA has, regrettably, not published any data on land prices since early 2011.

59. Cullingworth and Nadin (2006) has a good discussion of the history.

60. A. Crook et al. 2010. The incidence, value and delivery of planning obligations in England in 2007/08. Department for Communities and Local Government.

61. Sir John Harman (Chair, Local Housing Delivery Group). 2012. Viability testing local plans. Home Builders Federation/Local Government Association (June).

62. Homes and Communities Agency. 2013. Land development and disposal plan, 2013/14 update (June).

63. T. Leunig and J. Swaffield. 2007. Cities unlimited. Policy Exchange.

64. A. Hull and G. Cooke. 2012. Together at home. Institute for Public Policy Research (June).

65. Lord Matthew Taylor sets out a coherent case for this in his submission to the 2014 Wolfson Prize.